Fitness Professionals' Guide to Sports Nutrition and Weight Management

Laura J. Kruskall, Ph.D., R.D., CSSD

ISBN: 978-1-60679-102-8
Library of Congress Control Number: 2010924870

Cover design: Karen McGuire
Book layout: Bean Creek Studio
Front cover photo: iStockphoto/Thinkstock

Healthy Learning
P.O. Box 1828
Monterey, CA 93942
www.healthylearning.com

This book is dedicated to all of my family members who have supported, encouraged, and inspired me throughout my life, and to my mentors who have given me the knowledge and guidance to at long last publish my first book. Nick, Mom, Grannie, and Uncle Will, without all of you my education would not have been possible and I would not have been able to live my dream of educating and mentoring those who have the same passion for nutrition and fitness as I do.

Dedication

Acknowledgments

I want to thank my husband, Nick (an exercise physiologist and ACSM Certified Health Fitness Specialist), for his role in providing a fitness professional's perspective on the content and usefulness of this book, as well as providing proofreading and editorial functions throughout.

Contents

Fitness Professionals' Guide to Sports Nutrition and Weight Management is designed to be a resource for fitness professionals who want to better understand the basic factors involved in sound nutrition. The first part of the book explains what constitutes credible information on nutrition and details where fitness professionals can find such information.

The book also defines an acceptable scope of practice for fitness professionals concerning nutrition and explains how giving sound nutritional advice can differ from practicing as a dietitian. In that regard, dietary guidelines and information that are appropriate for fitness professionals to share with their clients are covered in a step-by-step manner.

In addition, the book explores the various energy systems that power the body and examines the basics of digestion. The factors that affect digestion, as well as the primary role of each organ involved in the process, are discussed. A detailed look at each of the various essential nutrients is also included.

The second part of the book looks at the impact of energy balance on weight management. The components of energy expenditure and how they can be collectively assessed are discussed, as are the essential points of concern about body composition. This part of the book also reviews the basic principles of sound weight management and explains what does and does not constitute a sound strategy for losing weight. The final chapter in this part discusses disordered eating, including the role that a fitness professional can play in helping someone who suffers from an eating disorder.

The third part of the book features answers to a series of commonly asked questions concerning sports nutrition and weight management. Each response, framed within the appropriate scope of practice for fitness professionals, is based on the most up-to-date information available. The focus of this part of the book is helping fitness professionals who want to clarify or better understand the nutrition-related issues that are relevant to their clients.

The Companion DVD

Fitness Professionals' Guide to Sports Nutrition and Weight Management also includes a companion DVD that features three separate videos on a single disc. The first video, *MyPyramid: USDA's Food Guidance System*, explains how this system can be used to help individuals make healthy food choices and be physically active every day. The second video, *Food Labels and Dietary Supplements: Understanding the Basics*, reviews the key factors involved in these two critical nutrition-related areas. The final video, *Healthy Grocery Shopping Tips*, details information, ideas, and insights that can enhance a person's ability to make nutritionally sound decisions when shopping for groceries.

Challenge and Change

When I first set forth to write *Fitness Professionals' Guide to Sports Nutrition and Weight Management*, my most daunting task was to compile a book that featured cutting-edge information on the key nutrition-related issues facing fitness professionals and to author it in such a way that the information was relatively easy to understand and apply.

Furthermore, I wanted this book to provide fitness professionals with a clear understanding of what constitutes an appropriate scope of practice when dispensing advice concerning nutrition and weight management. To the extent that this book has accomplished that goal and has enabled fitness professionals to better understand how they can effectively get their clients to modify their behavior, when needed, with regard to sports nutrition and weight management, then the time and energy expended to write this book will have been well worth the effort.

L.K.

NUTRITION BASICS EVERY FITNESS PROFESSIONAL SHOULD KNOW

Part I

iStockphoto/Thinkstock

1

The Fitness Profession and Credible Nutrition Information

Why Should Fitness Professionals Study Nutrition?

One of the primary goals of all fitness professionals should be to do whatever they can to enhance the physical well-being of their clients. In fact, several of the most common causes of death in the United States have a nutritional component, including both the number one cause of death, cardiovascular disease, and certain types of cancer, hypertension, and uncontrolled diabetes. Accordingly, it is imperative that fitness trainers have at least a basic understanding of the interaction between diet and disease. Beyond overall health promotion, fitness professionals are often asked to develop training programs to help improve fitness and athletic performance. Such exercise regimens tax various components of human metabolism to differing degrees. In turn, the practitioner without a working knowledge of nutrition runs the risk of designing exercise programs that cannot be sustained without adequate nourishment. Consequently, it is essential for fitness professionals to understand the basic classification, function, and metabolism of nutrients, the nutrient requirements of humans, and the relationship between nutrients and health and performance.

Nutrition is a relatively young science, with advances in knowledge being discovered and published on a regular basis. Nutrition is also a very expansive topic that features a relatively wide range of findings and information—from established guidelines that are based on significant scientific support to theories that are speculation at this point due to the early stages of research attendant to them. For example, information about the nutrient content of foods and specific nutrient recommendations for healthy individuals is fairly well-established. On the other hand, the role of antioxidants in the disease process or the exact amount of dietary protein needed for maximal protein synthesis before, during, and after an exercise training bout is not clearly defined.

A relatively novel area in the study of nutrition is the relationship between diet and physical activity, an association that is often referred to as sports nutrition. Similar to the study of nutrition in general, significant scientific support exists for certain nutrient recommendations during different types of physical activity, while relatively minimal research has been undertaken in other areas of nutrition. For example, an abundance of data exists that examines the impact of carbohydrates on endurance exercise performance. As a result, guidelines have been established regarding a person's carbohydrate needs to support various forms of physical activity. On the other hand, insufficient scientific support exists for many of the sports supplements purporting to enhance athletic performance.

An abundance of data exist that examines the impact of carbohydrates on endurance exercise performance.

iStockphoto/Thinkstock

Credible Nutrition Information

Nutrition information can be obtained from several sources. Many of these sources are credible and supported by significant scientific evidence, while others are anecdotal and not based on any scientific research whatsoever. In this instance, scientific support refers to the fact that several research studies have been completed and published to establish a specific theory. Groups of experts in the field read and interpret the data from the studies and then form guidelines for the public. Examples of this process include the current Dietary Reference Intakes (the guidelines for the quantity of nutrients that healthy individuals should consume) or the various position papers that have been published by a professional organization about a particular topic.

The most highly regarded type of nutrition information is evidence-based. Practitioners of evidence-based nutrition attempt to integrate the best available guidelines and scientific evidence with their own professional expertise and their client's personal preferences and values. Fitness practitioners often use evidence-based guidelines during fitness assessments, exercise testing, and program design. Similar guidelines exist for nutrient recommendations for healthy individuals. While these guidelines should be followed, the extent to which a fitness professional can legally implement them is limited. This particular issue will be addressed in greater detail throughout this book.

How to Find Credible Information

All sorts of information are instantly available on the World Wide Web. In fact, the Internet is probably the first place people visit when they want information about a topic. The problem with such widespread availability of information is that no built-in filter exists that excludes sources that are incorrect. Accordingly, care must be taken to identify which sources are credible and which are not. The following guidelines can help increase the likelihood that the information you are reading has credible scientific support:

- Choose information and guidelines that were developed and published by a governmental organization. Examples include the *Dietary Guidelines for Americans* or MyPyramid.gov. These sites will be discussed in a later chapter.

- Navigate to websites hosted by a professional organization that is widely respected by practitioners in the field. A number of professional organizations provide nutrition-related information for professionals and consumers. A leading professional organization in the field of nutrition and dietetics is the American Dietetic Association (www.eatright.org).

- Give higher credence to peer-reviewed journal articles over non-peer-reviewed sources. In order for a manuscript to get published in a peer-reviewed journal, it must go through a formal review process by other experts in the field. This process ensures that published research studies have been scrutinized by impartial experts for the soundness of the research methods utilized, and that the conclusions of the authors are supported by their research findings. In general, journals with the strongest peer-review process tend to have the best reputations and are considered the most credible.

Where to Find Peer-Reviewed Journal Articles

Peer-reviewed journal articles can be found by searching databases such as PubMed, a database of biomedical articles from the National Library of Medicine (www.pubmed.gov). How do you know if an article is peer-reviewed? Because most of the articles in a PubMed search are from peer-reviewed journals, if this database contains the article, then the article has likely been peer-reviewed. In addition, many databases have an option that allows the user to search only peer-reviewed sources. When in doubt, you can always seek the assistance of a medical librarian at a college or university.

Another way to ascertain if an article is peer-reviewed is to determine who is on the editorial board of the journal in which the article appears. Most journals list the names, credentials, and professional affiliations of each editorial board member at the beginning of each issue. If the editorial board members are heavily credentialed experts in the field and have affiliations with widely respected institutions and organizations, then it is likely that the journal only publishes peer-reviewed research. Because even peer-reviewed journals vary in quality, fitness practitioners should seek the advice of a medical librarian whenever the quality of a particular journal is in question.

Types of Research Studies and Journal Articles

Most studies in the health sciences are case studies, epidemiological studies, or experimental studies. Case studies are published observations of a person or group of people. While this approach may provide helpful information for generating research ideas, it is considered a weak form of scientific support.

Epidemiological studies, on the other hand, report associations or correlations between two variables. Such studies generally involve relatively large populations. For example, such a study might determine that populations that consume large amounts of fruits and vegetables may be at lower risk for developing certain diseases. While these types of studies can be helpful in understanding relationships, they typically do not control many of the variables that may be related to certain outcomes.

The strongest category of studies is experimental. Within this category, randomized double-blind, placebo-controlled experiments tend to produce the best evidence. Randomization means that in order to avoid bias, the research subjects in the study were randomly assigned to a particular treatment group. Double-blind refers to the fact that both the principal investigator and the subjects do not know which treatment they are receiving. Placebo-controlled indicates that one group receives the treatment, while the other gets an identical substitute without the treatment. Accordingly, a randomized, double-blind, placebo-controlled study essentially ensures that any differences between treatment groups can reasonably be assumed to have been caused by the treatment itself and not by any uncontrolled factors. As such, this type of research is a step above epidemiological studies, which can only suggest a correlation between two variables.

Different types of articles are contained in a database. A *primary research article* is one in which a study was conducted and the results of that study are published. Articles within this clarification are generally broken down into the following sections:

- *Abstract*: Provides a summary of the study.
- *Introduction*: Describes what has been researched and published previously and usually states the purpose of the current study.
- *Methods*: Details the research, animal model, or human subjects descriptively, the intervention, and the statistical analyses used in the study.
- *Results*: Describes the findings of the study, including their statistical significance. Data tables or figures are frequently used to illustrate the results of a particular study.
- *Discussion*: Includes speculation from the authors about the results of the study and compares the results of this study to other published papers in the field. The strengths and limitations of the study, as well as future directions for relevant research, may be discussed.

A *review article* is a summary of previous studies that have been published up to the point in time that this particular article was published. Such an article offers a reasonably appropriate starting point when investigating a particular topic for the first time. Review articles contain a comprehensive set of references that can also be read to identify additional details and descriptions of the original research.

A *meta-analysis* is similar to a review article, except in this instance the authors take data from other primary research articles and statistically re-analyze it to put the results on a level playing field. This type of paper also includes a comprehensive list of references for possible use at a later date.

When reviewing literature, it is important to avoid focusing on one article or a small sub-set of articles because critical research findings could be missed that could otherwise contradict any misleading conclusions. In order to obtain a complete picture of the evidence, it is best to start with a recent review article and expand the search according to the findings of the review article. On the other hand, if you are looking for information on a relatively new supplement, a review article from which to begin may not even exist. In that case, the best solution is to read all the original research articles and come to a reasonable conclusion based on the information in those sources.

When reading research articles, it is important to consider a number of factors before drawing any conclusions, including:

- Was the study conducted on animals or humans? It is important to keep in mind that data from animal studies cannot always be applied or extrapolated to humans.
- What study population was used? For example, results from investigations involving young men may not be applicable to women or older individuals.
- How many research subjects were used? Absolute conclusions should not be drawn from the findings of a single study that was conducted on a relatively small number of people. In reality, larger studies are needed to confirm conclusions that are made from the results of smaller studies. Unfortunately, the media often publicizes the results of a single study and implies that its findings are fact.
- Was the study a randomized, double-blind, placebo-controlled study?
- Does the study include "preliminary" or "unpublished" data? Such information should be viewed with caution. While preliminary results may be interesting, significant scientific agreement or consensus must be realized before sound guidelines can be established from the data. It should also be noted that research results "published" on a website or in a newsletter do not offer the same level of credibility as a peer-reviewed journal article.

It is important to recognize that nutrition is a relatively young science. In reality, it takes time to establish scientific knowledge. As such, it is essential that fitness practitioners emphasize to their clients that some areas of nutrition have clear, established guidelines, while other aspects of nutrition are still being researched—topics on which solid conclusions cannot yet be drawn.

It is important to recognize that nutrition is a relatively young science.

Scope of Practice

❑ The Importance of the Fitness Professional in Giving Sound Nutrition Advice

Because fitness and nutrition are closely interrelated, the role that fitness practitioners should play when addressing nutrition-related issues is sometimes unclear. In reality, fitness professionals are often the front-line personnel when dealing with individuals who want to learn about nutrition. Since most people seeking healthy lifestyle changes may see a fitness professional several times before seeking the advice of a qualified dietitian, it is likely that fitness practitioners will be asked numerous questions about nutrition.

It is important that fitness professionals provide their clients with current, accurate information about the role of sound nutrition in good health, without violating existing state laws that are designed to limit the nutrition information that fitness practitioners can legally and responsibly share with their clients. In general, fitness professionals can legally offer their clients a solid base of general nutrition in two primary ways—by providing evidence-based information and by identifying and explaining nutrition misinformation. Without this guidance, their clients may seek advice from other individuals (e.g., supplement store clerks) or from possibly even less credible sources (e.g., random websites).

❑ State Licensure in Nutrition and Dietetics

In many states, anybody can call himself a "nutritionist," a "nutrition professional," a "nutrition counselor," or a similar term. These terms may or may not be legally defined, a situation that varies from state to state. Thirty states have enacted laws licensing the profession of dietetics. In these situations, state statutes explicitly define the scope of practice concerning dietetics. Improperly engaging in the practice of dietetics in these states is illegal and can lead to misdemeanor or felony charges, resulting in penalties ranging from a cease-and-desist order to fines and imprisonment. Nineteen states have statutory certification in dietetics. In these instances, using certain nutrition-related titles is limited, but practicing in the area of nutrition may not be restricted. It is very important for fitness professionals to check the statutes in their states concerning what they may be legally permitted to do with regard to dispensing nutrition information. If needed, they should seek legal counsel before giving nutrition advice to any clients.

The term "Registered Dietitian" is a legal credential and cannot be used unless that credential was earned and maintained. The Commission on Dietetic Registration of the American Dietetic Association is the governing body for this credential. In order to become a Registered Dietitian, an individual must:
- Complete a didactic program in dietetics (DPD)—a program accredited by the Commission on Accreditation for Dietetics Education (CADE) of the American Dietetic Association.* A bachelor's degree is required in the

*For more information on this process or for a list of programs, visit the CADE website at: www.eatright.org/cade.

process and often the DPD and the bachelor's degree are completed concurrently. The DPD currently has 31 extensive foundational knowledge requirements and learning outcomes that must be mastered in the program.

- Complete a CADE-accredited, supervised practice experience (dietetic internship). This requirement involves a minimum of 1200 hours of experience, in which the dietetic intern demonstrates competencies in the areas of food and beverage management, community nutrition, and clinical dietetics.
- Pass the national registration examination for dietitians.
- Once the Registered Dietitian credential is granted, it must be maintained through continuing education and a professional development portfolio.

Most fitness certifications require some nutrition knowledge. It is important for all fitness practitioners to be able to discuss accurate nutrition information with their clients, without practicing within the scope of a Registered Dietitian. Similar to many facets of the health, wellness, and exercise professions, dietetics is a specialty practice area. To be completely safe and within legal limits, fitness professionals should limit discussions with their clients to general, non-medical information. Any response beyond this level should be given only after referring to state statutes and/or seeking the advice of legal counsel.

Summary

Fitness professionals owe it to their clients to have a basic understanding of nutrient classification, function, and metabolism; how nutrition affects health and disease; and, most importantly, how dietary intake impacts physical activity and human performance. The field of nutrition and dietetics is broad and seemingly endless, with new knowledge being published daily. While it is not expected, or appropriate, for fitness professionals to conduct in-depth nutrition assessments or to provide any sort of medical nutrition therapy, they are expected to discern credible from noncredible nutrition information. They should also be able to explain such information to their clients in a manner that is comprehensible and that allows the clients to make informed decisions about what to consume in their diets. The primary role of fitness professionals is that of educators, rather than practitioners, and it is important that they practice within their scope of expertise. Practicing dietetics is outside the scope of expertise of all fitness certifications, and to do so can expose fitness professionals to legal liability should something go awry due to advice that they have given. However, having knowledge of and disseminating general nonmedical nutrition information is part of most reputable fitness certifications, and clients expect fitness professionals to have this knowledge. Care must be taken to identify situations that require advanced dietetics proficiency and such cases should be referred to a registered dietitian.

2

Dietary Guidelines That Fitness Professionals Can Use

Giving Sound Advice Versus Practicing as a Dietitian

As discussed in the previous chapter, competent fitness professionals should be willing and able to provide accurate dietary guidelines for their clients, without violating state law by either performing nutrition assessments or giving inappropriate nutrition information. The information and guidelines presented in this chapter have been prepared for the purpose of educating the general populace. Accordingly, they can be used by all fitness professionals when dealing with healthy clients. It is critical to understand that these guidelines are just what their name implies—they are general principles that, if followed by the average person, would likely promote overall physical well-being.

Fitness professionals, unless they are also licensed or Registered Dietitians, should only attempt to educate their clients about the aforementioned dietary guidelines and general principles. Fitness professionals who are not also Registered Dietitians or licensed by the state where they practice, should never perform any type of nutrition assessment or meal planning activities for their clients, especially if a client has a disease or symptoms of disease. Such functional tasks fall under the umbrella known as medical nutrition therapy (MNT), which in many states can only be legally provided by licensed or Registered Dietitians. Few, if any, reputable fitness certifications require the practitioner who is being certified to be competent at either assessing nutritional status or prescribing diets for individuals. Since professional organizations establish the general standards of care for the fitness industry, anyone who practices outside their scope of knowledge and abilities can potentially be deemed negligent by a court of law and liable for damages. A number of cases exist where personal trainers have been sued and were found liable for damages because they created meal plans and/or recommended nutritional supplements to their clients that were inappropriate and caused serious adverse effects.

Nutrient Classification and Basic Functions

There are six primary categories of nutrients: carbohydrates, lipids, proteins, vitamins, minerals, and water. These nutrients are also classified into two distinct groupings, each determined by the quantity of a particular nutrient that is needed in the diet. Macronutrients are those nutrients that are required in larger quantities and include carbohydrates, lipids, proteins, and water. Micronutrients, on the other hand, which are only needed in small or trace amounts, include vitamins and minerals.

Macronutrients are known as the energy nutrients because they contain stored energy. Macronutrients are basically packets of potential energy that when consumed and digested, become energy reservoirs that fuel all bodily functions. The energy content of food is quantified using the unit of measurement known as the kilocalorie. While the general public often uses the term "calorie" to describe the energy content of a food item, the correct nomenclature that should be used is kilocalorie. For example, when a layperson says "there are 200 calories in a donut," what that individual really means is that there are 200 kilocalories in a donut. Throughout this book, the term "calorie" is frequently used instead of "kilocalorie," although the latter term is technically correct.

The energy content of food is quantified using the unit of measurement known as the kilocalorie.

Without vitamins and minerals, human metabolism could not occur at a rate sufficient to sustain life.

The primary function of carbohydrates is to provide fuel to working organs (e.g., brain and skeletal muscle). Lipids provide protection for the organs and insulation for the body, but one of its primary functions, like carbohydrates, is to provide fuel for the body. Unlike carbohydrates and lipids, protein has several non-energy functions. Some proteins provide the structural framework in bone, skin, and cell membranes. Other proteins perform enzymatic (kinase, phosphorylase), transport (albumin, hemoglobin), immune (antibodies), and communication (hormones, neurotransmitters) functions. Like the other macronutrients, protein can also be metabolized and used as an energy source to fuel the body, although this is not an ideal function of protein. Because proteins are best utilized for growth, maintenance, and repair of the body, they normally have only a minimal contribution as a fuel source. In the nourished, non-diseased state, protein generally contributes approximately 5% of an individual's total-body energy needs.

Vitamins and minerals are involved in the process of energy metabolism, but are not considered energy nutrients because they contain no calories. However, vitamins and minerals play a critical role in metabolism in that they often function as co-enzymes that allow specific metabolic processes to occur. As such, without vitamins and minerals, human metabolism could not occur at a rate sufficient to sustain life.

Water is a macronutrient with various functions, including being a solvent, a transport medium, a lubricant, and a regulator of body temperature. Water is so critical to life that even small amounts of body water loss can be detrimental to normal function, particularly during exercise activities lasting for an extended period of time. Later sections of this book will include guidelines on fluid replenishment during various forms of exercise.

Dietary Guidelines for Americans

The *Dietary Guidelines for Americans* (2005) are published by the United States Department of Agriculture (USDA) and the Department of Health and Human Services (www.health.gov/dietaryguidelines). The *Guidelines* are updated every five years and are designed to meet nutrient requirements, promote health, and prevent disease in people over the age of two. The *Guidelines*, which are developed by experts and are based on current scientific knowledge, are very general and are not designed to replace medical nutrition therapy in a person with disease. In addition, the *Guidelines* do not apply to active individuals. The key recommendations for each of the nine emphasis areas within the *Guidelines* are summarized in the following section, along with tips on how a fitness practitioner can contribute to a client's understanding of the *Guidelines* (the USDA's website provides more detailed information on each of the guidelines).

❑ Guideline #1: Adequate Nutrients Within Calorie Needs

- Consume a variety of nutrient-dense foods and beverages within and among the basic food groups, while choosing foods that limit the intake of saturated and trans fats, cholesterol, added sugars, salt, and alcohol.
- Meet recommended intakes within energy needs by adopting a balanced eating pattern, such as the one presented in *USDA Food Guide: Steps to a Healthier You* or the Dietary Approaches to Stop Hypertension (DASH) eating plan.
- Keep in mind that Americans often over-consume energy and some nutrients like saturated fats, trans fats, and sugars, while under-consuming other nutrients like omega-3 fatty acids, calcium, and potassium. As such, fitness professionals should teach the concept of "empty calories" versus nutrient dense foods to their clients.

❑ Guideline #2: Weight Management

- To maintain body weight in a healthy range, balance calories from foods and beverages with calories expended. Fitness professionals should recommend appropriate levels of physical activity to match their clients' dietary intakes and help them reach their body-weight goals in a safe and effective manner.
- Make relatively small decreases in the amount of food and beverage calories consumed and increase the level of physical activity undertaken in order to prevent gradual weight gain over time.
- The prevalence of obesity in both adults and children has doubled over the past two decades. It is estimated that approximately 65% of the population is classified as overweight (BMI 25-30), and approximately 30% is classified as obese (BMI > 30). As such, fitness practitioners have a responsibility to discuss with their clients the relationship between overweight and obesity and the development of chronic disease.

❏ Guideline #3: Physical Activity

- Engage in regular physical activity and reduce sedentary activities to promote health, psychological well-being, and a healthy body weight.

- Engage in at least 30 minutes of moderate-intensity physical activity, above usual activity, at work or home on most days of the week, in order to reduce the risk of chronic disease in adulthood.

- Note that for most people, greater health benefits can be obtained by engaging in physical activity of more vigorous intensity or longer duration.

- Engage in approximately 60 minutes of moderate- to vigorous-intensity activity on most days of the week, while not exceeding caloric intake requirements, in order to help manage body weight and prevent gradual, unhealthy body weight gain in adulthood.

- Participate in at least 60-90 minutes of daily moderate-intensity physical activity, while not exceeding caloric intake requirements, in order to sustain weight loss in adulthood. Some people may need to consult with a healthcare provider before participating in this recommended level of activity.

- Achieve physical fitness by including cardiovascular conditioning, stretching exercises for flexibility, and resistance exercises or calisthenics for muscle strength and endurance.

- Keep in mind that since this guideline is not "dietary" in nature, it is one in which fitness professionals have the expertise. As such, fitness practitioners, when partnering with a Registered Dietitian (who often is not qualified to discuss exercise-training regimens in great detail), can be particularly helpful in implementing this guideline.

Fitness professionals should recommend appropriate levels of physical activity to match their clients' dietary intakes and help them reach their body-weight goals in a safe and effective manner.

❑ Guideline #4: Food Groups to Encourage

- Consume a sufficient amount of fruits and vegetables, while staying within energy needs. Two cups of fruit and 2½ cups of vegetables per day are recommended for a reference 2,000-calorie intake, with higher or lower amounts depending on the calorie level. Fitness professionals should encourage clients to eat fruits and vegetables for several reasons: 1) they contain fiber; 2) they tend to be low in calories (especially vegetables); 3) they contain vitamins and minerals, some of which are rich in antioxidants; and 4) they contain phytochemicals, which are biologically active compounds found in plants that may play a role in health promotion and the prevention of disease.

- Choose a variety of fruits and vegetables each day. In particular, select from all five vegetable subgroups (dark green, orange, legumes, starchy vegetables, and other vegetables) several times a week.

- Consume three or more ounce-equivalents of whole-grain products per day (depending on energy needs), with the rest of the recommended grains coming from enriched or whole-grain products. In general, at least half the grains should come from whole grains. Whole-grain products are rich in fiber and other nutrients.

- Consume three cups per day of fat-free or low-fat milk or equivalent milk products, depending on energy needs. Non-fat or low-fat dairy foods are rich in protein and calcium. Calcium is an important nutrient for bone health and may play other roles (which are discussed in a later chapter). Encourage clients to make simple changes, like adding vegetables to pizza instead of high-fat meat toppings or use whole-grain bread or pasta instead of that made from white flour.

Medioimages/Photodisc

Individuals should select from all five vegetable subgroups (dark green, orange, legumes, starchy vegetables, and other vegetables) several times a week.

Incorporating healthy fats into the diet may help keep blood lipids favorable and be beneficial for certain conditions (e.g., metabolic syndrome).

❑ Guideline #5: Fats

- Consume less than 10% of calories from saturated fatty acids and less than 300 mg/day of cholesterol, and keep trans fatty acid consumption as low as possible. Regularly consuming foods high in saturated and trans fats may increase the risk of developing cardiovascular disease.
- Keep total fat intake between 20 and 35% of calories, with most fats coming from sources of polyunsaturated and monounsaturated fatty acids, such as fish, nuts, and vegetable oils. Incorporating healthy fats into the diet may help keep blood lipids favorable and be beneficial for certain conditions (e.g., metabolic syndrome).
- When selecting and preparing meat, poultry, dry beans, and milk or milk products, make choices that are lean, low-fat, or fat-free.
- Limit intake of fats and oils high in saturated and/or trans fatty acids, and choose products low in such fats and oils.

❑ Guideline #6: Carbohydrates

- Choose fiber-rich fruits, vegetables, and whole grains as often as possible.
- Choose and prepare foods and beverages with little added sugars or caloric sweeteners, such as amounts suggested by the *USDA Food Guide: Steps to a Healthier You* and the DASH eating plan.
- Reduce the incidence of dental caries by practicing good oral hygiene and consuming sugar- and starch-containing foods and beverages less frequently.

❏ Guideline #7: Sodium and Potassium

- Consume less than 2,300 mg (approximately one tsp. of salt) of sodium per day.
- Choose and prepare foods with little salt. At the same time, consume potassium-rich foods, such as fruits and vegetables.
- Keep in mind that one of the top sources of sodium in the American diet is processed foods. Fitness practitioners should encourage their clients to eat whole foods whenever possible and limit the consumption of processed foods. Research has shown that diets lower in sodium and higher in potassium (e.g., from fruits) may help maintain or improve blood pressure. High blood pressure increases an individual's risk for stroke and kidney disease.

❏ Guideline #8: Alcoholic Beverages

- If you choose to drink alcoholic beverages, do so sensibly and in moderation (defined as the consumption of up to one drink per day for women and up to two drinks per day for men).
- Keep in mind that alcoholic beverages should not be consumed by some individuals, including those who cannot restrict their alcohol intake, women of childbearing age who may become pregnant, pregnant and lactating women, children and adolescents, individuals taking medications that can interact with alcohol, and those with specific medical conditions.
- Alcoholic beverages should be avoided by individuals who are engaging in activities that require attention, skill, or coordination, such as driving or operating machinery.
- Be aware that alcohol contains calories and consuming too much alcohol may impair nutritional status and increase the risk for developing certain cancers, high blood pressure, stroke, and liver disease. Some data suggest that consuming one or two drinks per day may be beneficial to health. On the other hand, limiting alcohol will make room in the diet for more nutrient-dense foods.

Fitness practitioners should encourage their clients to eat whole foods whenever possible and limit the consumption of processed foods.

Consuming too much alcohol may impair nutritional status and increase the risk for developing certain cancers, high blood pressure, stroke, and liver disease.

❑ Guideline #9: Food Safety

- Consuming foods free from harmful levels of organisms and contaminants is essential for health.
- Food-borne illness can result in severe gastrointestinal stress and can even cause death.
- Additional information about food safety can often be found at a local governmental health agency, which is referred to in some states as a "health district"; in fact, many such organizations offer education and certifications in this area.

❑ Additional Resources Provided by the USDA ✳

The USDA website has many other features that fitness trainers can use in their practice. The following is a non-exhaustive list of some of these features:
- Scientific details for each of the nine guidelines
- Food sources of selected nutrients
- Reproducible worksheets promoting various healthy pursuits
- Schedules to track food intake and physical activity
- Downloadable slideshow presentations on nutrition topics
- Tips for eating out and shopping

Food Labels

Pursuant to the Nutrition Labeling and Education Act of 1990, many packaged foods require a nutrition facts label. Some foods, like meat and poultry, fresh fruits and vegetables, and spices, are not required to have a label, because either they are not regulated by the FDA or they do not contain a significant quantity of nutrients. A number of individuals have found that understanding how to properly read a food label is a prerequisite for healthy eating. Appendix A1 contains an educational handout from the USDA that describes how to read and understand a standard food label.

In addition to the food label, many food manufacturers also make assertions, called nutrient content claims (NCC), about the quantities of certain nutrients in their food products. Since these claims are defined by the FDA, any product that uses an established NCC must contain the amount of nutrient defined by the NCC. For example, in order for a food label to use the term "fat-free," the product must have <0.05 g of fat per serving. When referring to a particular product, the terms "good source" and "high source" mean that a serving of that product must meet 10-19% or at least 20% of the Daily Value, respectively, for a particular nutrient.

Some foods, like meat and poultry, fresh fruits and vegetables, and spices, are not required to have a label, because either they are not regulated by the FDA or they do not contain a significant quantity of nutrients.

iStockphoto/Thinkstock

A product label is allowed to contain a health claim that diets low in saturated fat and cholesterol may reduce the risk of cardiovascular and/or heart disease, but it cannot say that this particular product will reverse existing atherosclerosis.

Another category of FDA-regulated statements on food labels, called health claims, refers to the relationship between a nutrient and a specific disease or health-related condition. For example, a product label is allowed to contain a health claim that diets low in saturated fat and cholesterol may reduce the risk of cardiovascular and/or heart disease. In contrast, a product label cannot say that this particular product will reverse existing atherosclerosis. The manufacturer is required to use intentionally ambiguous terms such as "may" or "might," because there is no known evidence that any particular food product has the ability to reverse the progression of disease. In addition, for a product to make a health claim about a particular nutrient (e.g., fiber, protein, vitamin A, vitamin C, calcium, or iron), it must be a "good source," before fortification, of that nutrient. Furthermore, a serving of the product cannot contain more than 13 g of fat, 4 g of saturated fat, 60 mg of cholesterol, or 480 mg of sodium.

Appendices B1 and B2 contain a short list of FDA-approved health claims and nutrient content claims; only those approved by the FDA may be used on food products. For a more extensive discussion, as well as a complete list of approved claims, visit the FDA website at www.fda.gov.

Dietary Reference Intakes

How much of a particular nutrient is needed in a typical diet? In order to answer that question, it is best to consult the Dietary Reference Intakes (DRIs). DRIs are the result of a collaborative effort between the Food and Nutrition Board of the Institute of Medicine in the United States and Health Canada. The following four specific terms fall under the umbrella term "DRI":

- Recommended Dietary Allowance (RDA): Defined as the amount of a nutrient that meets the needs of almost all individuals in a particular reference group (e.g., similar gender, age, pregnancy status). RDAs are based on the results of extensive scientific research.

- Adequate Intake (AI): Defined as the amount of a nutrient that is believed to satisfy the needs of almost all individuals in a reference group. This designation is somewhat less firm than RDA and implies that further research is needed for more definitive conclusions.

- Estimated Energy Requirement (EER): Used to estimate the energy needs of an average person based on gender, height, weight, age, and physical-activity level.

- Upper Level (UL): Defined as the highest amount of a nutrient that can likely be consumed regularly without adverse health effects.

DRIs are designed to meet the needs of approximately 97-98% of a healthy population. Individuals with known disease cannot assume that consuming the DRI of particular nutrient will protect them from nutrient deficiency or overdose. Free copies of the DRIs are available for download on the USDA's website (www.usda.gov) and can be found in Appendix C2. The first two pages summarize micronutrient needs, the next two pages include the ULs, and the pages thereafter include the equations for estimating energy needs and the DRIs for macronutrients.

USDA MyPyramid Tool

As mentioned previously, meal planning is a type of medical nutrition therapy that in many states can legally be performed only by licensed or Registered Dietitians. As such, personal trainers should try to avoid designing personalized meal plans for their clients. Instead, practitioners should focus on helping their clients understand the healthy-eating guidelines that have been published by government agencies and well-respected professional organizations. One such tool distributed by the USDA, which can be found at www.mypyramid.gov, can safely be used by healthy individuals to design their own meal plans. Fitness professionals should learn this tool inside and out, so that they will be able to effectively teach their healthy clients about the site and encourage them to use the various features of the program detailed on the site. The materials on this website are free of charge.

Several practical things can be done with the resources that are on the USDA MyPyramid site. The most commonly used feature is the simple meal plan that can be created for healthy individuals. Under the "MyPyramid Plan" link, individuals enter their age, gender, weight, height, and physical-activity level. In turn, a generic meal plan is provided. Since this meal plan is created by the USDA, based on information provided directly by the client, there is no liability for the fitness practitioner. The meal plan itemizes the numbers of servings from each food group that should be consumed and also gives tips on serving sizes and other information on specific nutrients. As such, the primary role of fitness professionals is to help clients navigate the website and to accurately assess their physical-activity level, which many clients tend to overestimate.

The website also includes a section called "For Professionals" where additional useful information can be found. For example, this section features a printable chart, called "MyPyramid Food Intake Pattern Calorie Levels" (Appendix D2), that provides an estimate of an individual's daily energy needs based on age, gender, and activity level. This resource is a handy reference that can be used to quickly answer a common question that many individuals ask, specifically, "How many calories do I need?" The section also includes a chart, called "MyPyramid Food Intake Patterns" (Appendix D1), that lists the number of recommended servings from each food group for several different daily calorie needs. Finally, the section contains a series of worksheets that convert a specific daily calorie intake into a visual of how much that particular intake level represents in terms of real food. Telling someone to eat 2000 calories a

Jupiterimages

The primary role of fitness professionals is to help clients navigate the website and to accurately assess their physical-activity level, which many clients tend to overestimate.

day is different than showing him a picture of all the food items that encompass those calories.

The MyPyramid site also has an interactive feature called "MyPyramid Tracker" that allows users to create an account and track their progress over time. The site can produce two reports. The first report compares an individual's actual caloric intake to that recommended by MyPyramid to see how closely the user was able to mimic the diet recommended by the website. The second report converts the individual's self-reported dietary record into a nutrient analysis, which includes a comparison to recommendations or acceptable ranges. Another feature for those individuals who are interested in weight management is the energy balance history. Users can enter both dietary intakes and physical activities into the website in order to determine whether they are in energy balance over a period of time. Dietary intakes that exceed exercise expenditures will likely result in weight gain. This tool is designed to alert the user of energy imbalances so that corrective measures can be taken. This interactive involvement is not for everyone, however. Some clients may view it as a burden, while others may enjoy viewing their progress over time.

Supplement Regulation

❏ The Food and Drug Administration

Dietary supplements are regulated by the Office of Nutritional Products, Labeling, and Dietary Supplements of the Food and Drug Administration (FDA) (www.fda.gov). The Dietary Supplement Health and Education Act (DSHEA) of 1994 legally defined a dietary supplement as "a product (other than tobacco) added to the total diet that contains at least one of the following: a vitamin, mineral, amino acid, herb, botanical, or concentrate, metabolite, constituent, or extract of such ingredients or combination of any ingredient described above."

❏ Claims

Three categories of claims are used for dietary supplements. Nutrient content claims and health claims, as discussed previously for foods, are also approved for use by the FDA with dietary supplements. A third category, known as structure-function claims, while not approved by the FDA, allows manufacturers to imply that a supplement has health benefits. While the producer of the supplement may not use a specific disease name in any claim, the manufacturer may make broad generalizations concerning a particular supplement, such as "promotes glucose health." While such a statement does not use the term "diabetes," it does imply that the supplement may be used to help treat this disease. Claims falling under this category will have the following disclaimer somewhere on the label: "This statement has not been evaluated by the Food and Drug Administration. This product is not intended to diagnose, treat, cure, or prevent any disease." A good rule of thumb to follow in this regard is that if a product has this disclaimer on it its package label, it is quite possible that the efficacy and/or quality of the product are in doubt.

❑ Other Regulation Points

- Supplements are regulated like foods, not food additives or drugs. In order for a drug to be sold or a food additive to be used, it must undergo a lengthy period of testing. Supplements do not need FDA approval prior to marketing.

- Supplement labels do not have to include who should not take the supplement, what drugs it should not be taken with, or other warnings.

- The manufacturer must substantiate claims, but the DSHEA does not specify what this means nor does it require that this evidence be shared with anybody, including the FDA.

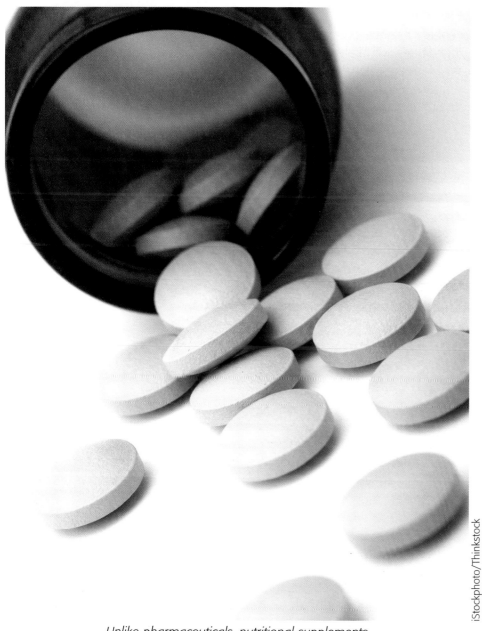

iStockphoto/Thinkstock

Unlike pharmaceuticals, nutritional supplements
are not evaluated by the FDA for content.

- The manufacturer is not required to record, report, investigate, or forward reports of illnesses to the FDA, nor does it have to disclose to the FDA or consumers any information it may have about the safety or purported benefits of the supplement.
- There are no limits on serving sizes (dosage) or potency. In other words, supplement manufacturers are permitted to sell a supplement containing a quantity equal to the DRI tolerable upper intake levels. Such a practice may be dangerous, because consumers will often take more than the recommended dose and will likely ingest the nutrient from other natural and fortified foods. As a result, it is not uncommon for users of a supplement to consume unsafe amounts.
- Unlike pharmaceuticals, nutritional supplements are not evaluated by the FDA for content. Supplements often contain more or less of an ingredient than what is stated on the label. No definitive way exists to ascertain how accurately a supplement label reflects the true content of the package. It is prudent to select supplements that are manufactured by companies that also produce pharmaceuticals, since it is likely that such companies have rigid standards for the production of highly regulated drugs.

❏ FDA's Dietary Supplements Current Good Manufacturing Practices

The FDA has proposed a plan to control the quality of dietary supplements sold to the public. This proposal will ultimately ensure that supplements are produced in a quality manner, do not contain contaminants or impurities, and are accurately labeled. This new rule is designed to achieve the following:
- Establishes protocols for ensuring quality control, designing and constructing manufacturing plants, and testing ingredients used in the manufacturing process, as well as the finished product
- Requires recordkeeping and responding to consumer complaints about the side effects of a particular product
- Calls for manufacturers to evaluate the identity, purity, strength, and composition of their supplements

An interim rule exists that exempts manufacturers from these requirements if they can prove that reduced testing would still ensure that all ingredients would be identified. The Current Good Manufacturing Practices and the interim final rule were effective in August 2007. The rule has a three-year phase-in for small businesses. Companies with more than 500 employees had until June 2008 to comply, those with less that 500 employees had until June 2009, and those with fewer than 20 employees had until June 2010.

The FDA is still perfecting this proposal, which may change with time. Keep in mind that this proposal is designed to control the quality of a particular product only and does not ensure that all claims are clear. Visit the FDA website regularly to keep current on these new regulations.

Discussing Supplements With Clients

❑ General Rules

While the Current Good Manufacturing Practices proposal helps address the issue of quality, it does not resolve issues about safety or efficacy. Fitness professionals still need to research any supplement before discussing it with their clients. Practitioners should use scientific evidence to fully inform their clients of the efficacy and safety of any supplement, and then allow each individual to decide whether or not to use a particular product. Because of potential liability, an allied health professional should avoid specifically recommending the use of any supplement.

When discussing the decision to take a supplement with a client, fitness practitioners should do the following:

- Remain non-judgmental when speaking with clients.
- Ask what products and dosages they are currently taking, why and for how long they have been consuming the supplement, and from whom they got the idea to take the product.
- Does a client's physician know about the consumption of the product? If not, encourage this communication, since supplements may interact with one another or with prescription or over-the-counter drugs.
- Discuss how supplements are regulated by the FDA. Many clients do not understand the process and assume that products on a store shelf must be regulated in a similar fashion to over-the-counter drugs.
- Be aware of possible media misinterpretation. It is important for fitness professionals to interpret the science. Be familiar with research design and methods and seek accurate conclusions, including statistical and clinical significance. In reality, a study may have statistical significance, but not much clinical significance. For example, if a weight-loss product resulted in a weight-loss difference of a few pounds, but was associated with negative side effects, this point should be considered in the discussion.

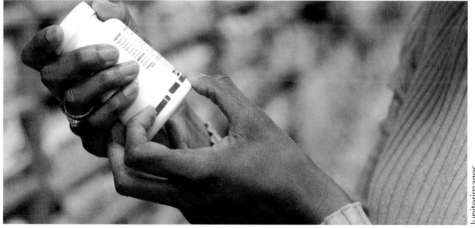

Jupiterimages

*Fitness professionals still need to research any
supplement before discussing it with their clients.*

- Accept that it is okay to not know about all supplements—there are so many on the market! It is perfectly acceptable to thoroughly research a product before answering any questions that an individual may have about a supplement.
- Don't assume that a lack of known side effects equates with safety. For example, just because there are no studies reporting side effects of a particular product does not mean that taking it is safe.
- Don't presume that products labeled as "natural" are inherently safe. For example, while oyster shell calcium is a natural product, it may be contaminated with mercury. Furthermore, many of the herbal supplements currently on the market are formulated and processed differently than they were in the past. As a result, many of the traditional uses of such supplements are no longer valid.
- Encourage clients to report any adverse reaction to their physician and the FDA (www.fda.gov/medwatch/report/consumer/consumer.htm or at 1-800-FDA-1088 or by fax 1-800-FDA-0178).

❏ Quality References

- *The Health Professional's Guide to Popular Dietary Supplements*, 3rd ed. The American Dietetic Association, 2007.
- PDR for Non-Prescription Drugs, Dietary Supplements, and Herbs. PDR Network, LLC, 2009.

❏ Independent Analysis of Quality

- Natural Products Association: www.naturalproductsassoc.org
- NSF International: www.nsf.org
- US Pharmacopeia: www.usp.org

❏ Useful Websites

- US Food and Drug Administration (FDA): www.fda.gov
- Office of Dietary Supplements: ods.od.nih.gov
- Tips for the Savvy Supplement User: www.cfsan.fda.gov/~dms/ds-savvy.html
- The Natural Pharmacist: www.iherb.com
- Consumerlab: www.consumerlab.com
- Supplement Watch: www.supplementwatch.com

Summary

Nutrition has a number of issues and aspects that involve general, non-medical nutrition information that fitness practitioners can share with their clients without practicing beyond their scope of expertise. The tools presented in this chapter can help guide and educate individuals to make informed choices about whether to consume nutritional supplements.

3

Energy Systems

Overview

Energy metabolism in its basic form involves breaking down large carbon, hydrogen, and oxygen-containing molecules into smaller ones, while simultaneously converting the energy released in this process into a form that powers all cellular activity, namely adenosine triphosphate (ATP).

At a level of exercise intensity that is not excessively high, humans are capable of producing enough ATP to fuel activity without fatigue, as long as sufficient energy substrates (carbohydrates, fats, and proteins) are readily available in the body. Short-term fatigue occurs when exercise intensity rises to levels that disturb the body's ability to break down and transport the energy from the carbon, hydrogen, and oxygen molecules that have been eaten. At a low level of exercise intensity, carbon-containing pyruvate is consistently oxidized to acetyl-CoA, provided sufficient oxygen is available. At the same time, hydrogen molecules are shuttled smoothly within cells by the compounds nicotinamide adenine dinucleotide (NAD) and flavin adenine dinucleotide (FAD). At such low exercise intensities, there are no metabolic byproducts that contribute to fatigue.

Short-term fatigue begins to occur when exercise intensity rises to a level that disturbs homeostasis. The primary culprit in this situation is the body's inability to inspire and transport oxygen to working muscles at a rate sufficient to keep up with the increased demand for ATP. When oxygen levels at the working muscle are insufficient due to rising exercise intensity, hydrogen molecules that normally bind with oxygen to form harmless water start to accumulate and eventually overwhelm the body's capacity to effectively transport NAD and FAD. As a result, hydrogen levels rise, blood acidity increases, and normal enzymatic activity is altered. Concurrently, pyruvate conversion to acetyl-CoA diminishes. Instead, the pyruvate accepts hydrogen molecules to form lactic acid. At this time, the only way to restore homeostasis in the body is to reduce the level of exercise intensity in order to enhance oxygen uptake and clear metabolic byproducts.

To state this more simply, the harder an individual works, the more demand there is for ATP production at the working muscle. At some point, because the ability to use oxygen to convert food into ATP cannot keep up with ATP demand, metabolic by-products (namely hydrogen molecules and lactate) begin to accumulate. In turn, the accumulation of hydrogen and lactate negatively affects metabolism and causes fatigue. Fatigue diminishes during recovery because ATP demand lessens to the point where ATP production can occur primarily through aerobic means. Based on this logic, it can be concluded that any training or nutritional intervention that can increase ATP production without also causing hydrogen and lactate to accumulate would likely result in an improvement in exercise performance.

Jupiterimages

The harder an individual works, the more demand there is for ATP production at the working muscle.

Energy Systems

❏ ATP-PC System

The most rapid method that the body uses to produce ATP is called the ATP-PC system. This system comes into play during explosive movements, such as a tennis serve or a power lift. While this system is rapid, it is very limited and only supplies ATP for up to 10 seconds. A critical molecule in the ATP-PC system is called phosphocreatine (PC), which is stored in skeletal muscle. PC is simply a molecule of creatine attached to a single phosphate molecule. PC can quickly replenish ATP by donating its phosphate to adenosine diphosphate (ADP). The reason that the ATP-PC system is so fleeting is because the pool of PC stored in the skeletal muscle is very limited. Once all of the PC molecules have donated their phosphate group to ADP, this system can no longer aid in ATP production until PC is replenished, which normally occurs during recovery. While creatine is found in meat products and therefore consumed regularly by many individuals, even people who consume no animal products (vegans) synthesize creatine internally. With regard to creatine, numerous studies suggest that it is possible to increase the amount of creatine stored in the muscles of some individuals via nutritional supplementation, a step which may lead to improved performance in sports that are heavily dependent on the ATP-PC system.

❏ Anaerobic Glycolysis

This system takes a six-carbon glucose molecule and breaks it down (oxidizes it) to two, three-carbon molecules called pyruvate. In the process, potential energy is generated in two ways. First, while glucose is being oxidized, hydrogen

Stockbyte

It should be noted that all metabolic systems work concurrently.

molecules are being removed. NAD receives these molecules, forms NADH, and transports hydrogen to a location called the "electron transport chain" (ETC), where ATP can be generated aerobically. Second, ATP is directly produced from the breakdown process of glucose to pyruvate. This pathway generates ATP fairly rapidly, and serves as the predominant energy system for one or two minutes of continuous activity.

❑ Aerobic Metabolism

This system, also known as oxidative phosphorylation, can break down carbohydrates, fats, or proteins. Unlike the other two energy systems, this system can supply ATP on a fairly limitless basis as long as macronutrients and oxygen are available. Acetyl-CoA, which is the broken-down form of both fats and glucose, is ultimately oxidized via aerobic metabolism. This compound combines with oxaloacetate to begin another pathway called the Krebs cycle. During the Krebs cycle, ATP is generated as acetyl-CoA is "converted" to oxaloacetate. In addition, many of the hydrogen molecules that are produced during the Krebs cycle are shuttled by NAD and flavin adenine dinucleotide (FAD) to the ETC. As the hydrogen molecules are passed along the chain, ATP is generated. Oxygen, which is at the end of the chain, binds with the hydrogen molecules to form water. As such, the ETC is the most efficient way that the human body produces ATP, because the system yields no metabolic by-products that produce fatigue.

This system can be used to generate ATP from all three energy nutrients, carbohydrates, lipids (fats), and proteins. Glucose and fatty acids enter the Krebs cycle in the form of acetyl-CoA. Amino acids can enter the pathway as acetyl-CoA, pyruvate, or other intermediates, depending on the particular amino acid.

Working Together

It should be noted that all metabolic systems work concurrently. One system does not "shut off" as another "turns on." In fact, all three systems are working at any given time. The relative contribution of each system will depend on the body's physiological need for ATP. For example, the ATP-PC system is used for very short-duration, high-intensity activities that last for a few seconds. Anaerobic glycolysis, which generates ATP fairly quickly from glucose, is used predominantly during the first minute or two of activity. Aerobic or oxidative metabolism, on the other hand, predominates during prolonged activities lasting up to several hours.

Summary

The usable form of energy in the human body is ATP, a compound that can be generated via three different systems. The body's demand for ATP dictates which system is predominately used at any given moment in time.

4

Digestion Basics

Overview

The digestive tract is a long hollow tube that begins in the mouth and ends at the anus. Nutrients from food must pass through the digestive tract to be absorbed into the bloodstream. Various stages of digestion occur at different parts of the digestive tract. A brief description of the primary digestive activities that occur along the length of the digestive tract can provide the basis for a better understanding of the digestive process.

The Digestive Process

❑ The Mouth

In the mouth, chewing serves to grind food into smaller pieces and increase the surface area upon which digestive enzymes can work. Many smaller pieces of food have a larger surface upon which enzymes can bind than does a single chunk of the same amount of that particular food. The larger surface area facilitates digestion, because virtually all digestive activities are driven by enzymatic reactions. In addition, saliva is released in the mouth. Saliva helps to moisten food, which allows for easier swallowing. Although food could be completely digested without first entering the mouth, gastrointestinal transit time is reduced when food is thoroughly masticated prior to swallowing.

❑ The Esophagus

Once food leaves the mouth, it travels to the stomach via a lengthy pipe in the digestive tract called the esophagus. While gravity helps the food travel to the stomach, it is not necessary due to involuntary, wave-like contractions along the entire digestive tract called peristalsis. Peristaltic contractions continually push food forward along the digestive tract. Reverse peristalsis, or vomiting, is the violent contractions of the stomach and esophagus in the opposite direction.

❑ The Stomach

The stomach is a holding reservoir that churns food and secretes digestive juices containing acids and enzymes. Food generally stays in the stomach for approximately two to four hours, although a number of factors can affect this timeframe. For example, liquids leave the stomach faster than solids. Carbohydrates exit more rapidly than proteins, and proteins exit more rapidly than lipids. High-fiber carbohydrates stay in the digestive tract longer than simple carbohydrates. This information can be useful in many circumstances. For example, during an athletic event where carbohydrate is needed fairly quickly, it is best to consume liquid carbohydrate or sports drinks. Conversely, for those people who are purposely restricting their caloric intake, it is a good idea to choose high-fiber, protein-rich meals that make an individual feel fuller for a longer period of time.

Stomach acid helps kill normal levels of bacteria that may be ingested with the food. On the other hand, even stomach acid cannot kill large quantities of bacteria and prevent food-borne illness caused by spoiled or improperly cooked food.

The stomach has an amazing ability to expand as food enters it. While an empty human stomach in an adult is roughly the size of a fist, a full stomach can expand to four times that size. Not surprisingly, when the size of an empty stomach is viewed in relation to the typical meal served in a restaurant in America, it is no wonder that most people leave a restaurant barely able to walk due to fullness.

After being churned and mixed with stomach acid and digestive enzymes, consumed food becomes a liquid substance known as chyme. Chyme remains in the stomach until it is ready to enter the next chamber of the digestive tract. Two valves in the stomach prevent chyme from exiting the stomach prematurely. These control measures are two narrow openings called sphincters that expand to allow food to pass through. One opening, called the esophageal sphincter, prevents food and acid from back flowing into the esophagus. When this process is not working properly, a person may be suffering from gastroesophageal reflux disease (GERD) and complain of "heartburn" symptoms. A second valve, known as the pyloric sphincter, prevents stomach chyme from entering the small intestine either prematurely or all at once. Normally, the stomach will gradually secrete the chyme into the small intestine.

❑ The Small Intestine

The small intestine is the primary site of digestion and absorption of nutrients into the body. In this part of the digestive tract, plentiful enzymes help break apart larger molecules into particles small enough to cross the intestinal cell wall into the bloodstream. Chyme typically remains in the small intestine for 3-10 hours, depending on its nutrient composition. Of all the macronutrients, fat takes the longest to digest.

The small intestine is more than just a smooth hollow tube. In fact, it contains villi and microvilli, or folds, that significantly increase the surface area to approximately 600 times that of a simple cylinder. The cells that line the intestinal wall have a very short lifespan and completely recycle every three to five days. The small intestine is a "use it or lose it" organ. If a person goes for long periods of time without eating, those cells die. In fact, they are not replaced because no demand exists for their use. The good news is that intestinal cells will regenerate over time with feeding. On the other hand, an individual cannot rapidly switch from fasting to overeating without some gastrointestinal distress. Until the cells grow back, nutrients will not be adequately absorbed, a situation that will often result in diarrhea. This information is particularly important for athletes in sports that have strict weight classes who attempt extreme dieting rituals in order to "make weight" before competitions.

George Doyle

An individual cannot rapidly switch from fasting to overeating without some gastrointestinal distress.

❑   The Large Intestine

Any nutrient that is not broken down small enough to cross the small intestinal wall will continue into the large intestine (colon). In a healthy person, only approximately 5% of a meal reaches the colon, an amount that includes some vitamins and minerals. Contents can remain in the large intestine for 24-72 hours, depending on the fiber and fluid content of the meal. The large intestine contains water, sodium, potassium, small amounts of undigested starches, and microflora, which are bacteria that help keep the colon healthy. Colon bacteria are also responsible for producing gas as a by-product of their digestion of fiber or other waste. Diets adequate in fluid and fiber generally result in stools that are soft and easily passed through the rectum. Diets inadequate in fluid and fiber may result in hard, dry stools.

Factors Affecting Digestion

Nervousness or stress can affect digestion time. In fact, no unequivocal rule exists as to whether stress speeds up or slows down digestion. For example, if an individual is nervous, consumed food may stay in the stomach longer than normal and produce an uncomfortable feeling. On the other hand, another person with the same level of stress might experience rapid digestion and the resultant case of diarrhea. This factor is an important reason to encourage athletically competitive individuals to get to know how their bodies react during competition.

Summary

Digestion is the process by which ingested food is broken down into smaller components and either stored within or excreted from the body. Digestion occurs throughout the length of the digestive tract that begins in the mouth and ends at the anus. Nutrients are digested and absorbed to different degrees at different locations along the digestive tract. The upper part of the digestive tract includes the mouth and esophagus and serves to crush large pieces of food and transport it to the stomach. The stomach is a harsh acidic environment that also contains enzymes to break down some proteins. Most digestion of fats, proteins, and carbohydrates occurs in the very long segment of the digestive tract called the small intestine. The large intestine, the lower part of the digestive tract, is where most water and electrolytes are reabsorbed into the body. The speed of digestion may be influenced by external factors, including the stress of athletic competition.

5

Carbohydrates

Carbohydrate Classifications

Carbohydrates, which contain the elements carbon, hydrogen, and oxygen, are classified according to size as monosaccharides, disaccharides, or polysaccharides. The smallest unit of a carbohydrate is called a monosaccharide and comes in one of three forms—glucose, fructose, and galactose. Glucose is often referred to as "blood sugar." Fructose, which is commonly found in fruit, is often referred to as "fruit sugar," while galactose typically exists in milk.

The next largest form of carbohydrate is called a disaccharide, a configuration that is simply the combination of two monosaccharides. The most common disaccharides in the human diet are sucrose, or "table sugar," lactose, or "milk sugar," and maltose. Sucrose molecules, which contain one fructose and one glucose molecule joined together, are abundant in the human diet. A lactose molecule combines a glucose molecule and a galactose molecule together. A maltose molecule connects two glucose molecules together.

The most complex form of carbohydrate is the polysaccharide, which involves a lengthy chain of monosaccharides joined together. Three of the most common polysaccharides are starch, fiber, and glycogen. Starch is the storage form of carbohydrate in plants, is abundant in the human diet, and is easily digested by the human body. Fiber also involves a chain of glucose molecules. Humans cannot break the bonds between these molecules, however, because they lack the appropriate enzymes to do so. As a result, fiber passes undigested through the gastrointestinal tract. Glycogen is the storage form of carbohydrate in animals and is found in both the liver and skeletal muscle. Unlike starch, which under a microscope looks fairly straight-chained, glycogen is highly branched. This attribute is physiologically beneficial because digestive enzymes work from the ends inward. Since glycogen has so many branches, the enzymes have a large surface area on which to work. As a result, glycogen can be broken down quite rapidly and digested by the human body.

Function of Carbohydrates

The primary function of carbohydrates in humans is to fuel organ activity, particularly the brain, heart, and skeletal muscle. In fact, some carbohydrates may also play structural roles at the cellular level. In reality, however, carbohydrate's role as a fuel source is absolutely vital.

Digestion and Metabolism of Carbohydrates

Carbohydrate digestion begins in the mouth with the aid of the enzyme salivary amylase. Salivary amylase starts digesting starch molecules by cleaving polysaccharide chains into smaller maltose molecules. Anyone who has placed a piece of bread in their mouth and noticed a sweet-like taste has experienced this process firsthand. Carbohydrate digestion in the mouth proceeds only to the level of the disaccharide. In fact, further digestion of disaccharides does not continue until they reach the small intestine. This situation exists because the acidic environment of the stomach interferes with the action of salivary amylase, an interplay that essentially stops digestion at this juncture.

The primary function of carbohydrates in humans is to fuel organ activity, particularly the brain, heart, and skeletal muscle.

Any form of carbohydrate not used as fuel or stored as glycogen will end up as adipose tissue triglyceride.

In the small intestine, the remainder of any consumed starch molecules is acted upon by pancreatic amylase, which degrades any remaining polysaccharides into disaccharides. Even disaccharides are too large to cross the intestinal wall and must be further split into monosaccharides before being assimilated into the bloodstream. Sucrase, lactase, and maltase are enzymes located in the intestinal wall that split disaccharides into their respective monosaccharides. The resulting monosaccharides cross the intestinal wall and travel via the bloodstream to the liver, where fructose and galactose are converted to glucose. Eventually, all ingested carbohydrate ends up in the liver as glucose.

The ultimate fate of ingested glucose depends on the metabolic demands of the body that exist at the time of digestion. One consequence is that glucose will be used as fuel by active organs. In addition, glucose can be converted to glycogen in the liver and skeletal muscle if glycogen stores are depleted in these locations. It should be noted that liver and muscle can only hold so much glycogen (strategies to enhance this situation are discussed in subsequent sections of this book). Finally, if organs are fueled properly and glycogen stores are full, the third destination for the ingested carbohydrate is storage as fat. The liver can take the excess glucose molecules, convert them to fatty acids, and store them as triglycerides in adipose tissue. Any form of carbohydrate not used as fuel or stored as glycogen will end up as adipose tissue triglyceride. This situation does not mean that this carbohydrate will remain in adipose tissue forever. More about this topic will be discussed in Chapter 10.

Normally, blood glucose levels are carefully maintained at a prescribed level by various internal-control mechanisms. For example, when blood glucose levels begin to fall, the body will respond by breaking down glycogen and releasing glucose into the bloodstream. Similarly, when blood glucose levels rise, the pancreas will secrete the hormone insulin into the blood to trigger the uptake of glucose into cells, thereby reducing blood glucose down to normal levels.

Carbohydrates and Health

❏ Carbohydrate Quality Levels

A popular myth exists that all carbohydrates are bad for health and that it is best to avoid these foods in the diet. This particular piece of fictitious lore is unfortunate because it is entirely untrue. What many people fail to realize is that carbohydrates come in different levels of quality. Poor-quality carbohydrates are made from processed, bleached flour. This type of carbohydrate usually lacks dietary fiber and may or may not lack other vitamins and minerals. Processed products are often "enriched," a term that refers to the fact that some of the nutrients lost while processing these items are added back before packaging. Products containing simple sugars have both carbohydrate and calories, but often lack other quality nutrients, such as fiber or vitamins and minerals.

High-quality carbohydrates, on the other hand, are generally found in unprocessed plants, legumes, and grains, items that contain abundant vitamins and minerals, as well as energy. High-quality carbohydrates also have a high level of indigestible dietary fiber, plant matter that helps keep the colon healthy and allows for stool to pass easily.

Plants also contain biologically active compounds called phytochemicals. Since phytochemicals are not required to sustain life, they are not nutrients. They are, however, believed to promote health and prevent disease. The scientific community has identified hundreds of phytochemicals, but their specific functions are not clear. While some data exists to support a relationship between the intake of phytochemicals and the prevention of disease, no established DRIs have been identified for these compounds. One example of a phytochemical is lycopene, which is the compound that makes tomatoes red and watermelon pink. Scientists believe that a positive relationship exists between the intake of lycopene and a reduced risk of prostate cancer. It is unclear, however, how much of this substance is needed in the diet. Furthermore, many supplement manufacturers are now isolating lycopene, putting it in a pill, and using the limited scientific data to market the product for health promotion. One of the main problems with relying on supplemental forms of vitamins, minerals, and phytochemicals is that these compounds may not work the same way when they are isolated from other components that are normally found in whole foods. For example, the lycopene in tomatoes may interact with other antioxidant nutrients or unidentified phytochemicals to have the protective effect described previously.

Eliminating carbohydrate-rich foods from the diet means that antioxidant nutrients and phytochemicals may not be consumed in optimal amounts for health and disease prevention. As such, it is important that individuals are aware of the health benefits of consuming quality carbohydrates in quantities that support energy balance.

Martin Poole

Eliminatinq carbohydrate-rich foods from the diet means that antioxidant nutrients and phytochemicals may not be consumed in optimal amounts for health and disease prevention.

❏ Relationship Between Fiber and Disease

Dietary fiber intake at appropriate levels may reduce the risk of certain diseases, such as colon cancer and diverticulosis. Diverticulosis is a medical condition that is common in older individuals and is characterized by pockets forming in the large intestine. These pockets generally develop after years of pressure from straining to defecate. With adequate fiber and fluid intake, stool passes easily and the risk of diverticulosis lessens. Diverticulitis occurs when diverticulosis pockets trap partially digested food and subsequently become infected and inflamed. This condition warrants the advice of a registered dietitian for treatment.

It is important to know that most Americans do not consume sufficient amounts of fiber in their diet. As such, one of the tasks for responsible fitness professionals is to encourage people to increase their intake of fiber by educating them about its benefits, as well as informing them of appropriate sources of dietary fiber. It should be noted that it is important to increase fiber intake gradually and to concurrently drink more fluids with enhanced fiber consumption; otherwise constipation may result.

The DRI for dietary fiber in adult individuals up to 50 years of age is 38 g per day for men and 25 g per day for women. The DRIs discussed in Chapter 2 and presented in Appendix C2 offer a complete list of fiber needs by life-stage and gender. Reading food labels is a simple way to determine the fiber content of various food products. In this situation, individuals should search for the term "whole grain" and also look at the nutrition facts panel on the product.

Individuals should also compare whole grain versus white products. With minor changes, individuals can significantly add fiber to their diets while still eating their favorite foods. For example, whole-grain pasta can have 6 g of fiber per serving versus one or less gram per serving in white pasta. Many cereals contain 10-15g of fiber in one-half to one cup. On the other hand, individuals should not be fooled by the term "whole wheat." For example, whole-wheat products may be brown in color because the flour is not bleached, although these products may not have much more fiber than a white-flour product.

❑　The Glycemic Index

Another myth that has gotten a great deal of publicity in recent years is one that states that foods with a high glycemic index (GI) are unhealthy, because they cause a rapid rise in blood sugar after consumption. Many people associate an elevated level of blood glucose, regardless of how transient the rise, with diabetes, obesity, and heart disease. The problem with this line of thinking is that many factors can impact the measurement of a food's GI that have nothing to do with how healthy a food is, such as crushing or mashing, cooking, addition of acids, variety and origin of growth, maturation/ripening, and the addition of other nutrients, such as protein or fat.

GI is a precisely defined measurement that indicates how quickly blood sugar rises in a fasting person in response to the consumption of exactly 50 g of available carbohydrate compared to a reference food, such as glucose or white bread. Foods are then loosely categorized as low, medium, or high, depending on how high blood sugar rises compared to the reference food. This measurement involves several limitations that make it unwise to use GI as a sole determinant of whether a food is unhealthy. One limitation is that the measurement is based on precisely 50 g of available carbohydrate, instead of on a standard serving size. For example, carrots have a relatively high GI. In reality, however, virtually no one would eat the large quantity of carrots that are necessary to induce a rapid rise in blood sugar. Another limitation of GI is that it is based on single foods in isolation and ignores the impact that eating other foods simultaneously can have on GI. As such, not very many people eat plain pasta or a plain potato, both of which have a high GI. On the other hand, if butter, cheese, sour cream, or even broccoli is added to that potato, or the potato is eaten in a meal with chicken, for example, then the GI is reduced. If some sauce, chicken, vegetables, or meat are added to that pasta, the GI is further attenuated. A third limitation of GI is that great inter-individual variability exists among people. For example, one person may develop hyperglycemia in response to orange juice, and yet not have the same response to pasta. In contrast, another individual may have the opposite reaction. Pasta causes that person to experience an increased level of blood glucose, while juice does not.

Barry Austin

Fitness professionals can play an important role in helping their clients manage their diabetes.

GI should be viewed as a tool and not a rule. For example, a marathon runner may want to eat a high-GI product, such as a sports drink, because that individual wants glucose to enter the bloodstream fairly rapidly to help spare glycogen during the activity, which lasts for several hours. On the other hand, foods should not be ruled out entirely simply because they have a high GI. Fitness professionals should teach their clients the limitations of GI and encourage them to know their own body's response to foods that have a high GI. It is important for fitness professionals to keep in mind that if they are working with clients who have diabetes or hypoglycemia, these individuals will likely require specific medical nutrition therapy and the services of a registered dietitian. In such situations, it is important that fitness professionals work closely with a dietitian, given that the exercise regimen that they recommend can have a significant impact on the client's blood glucose level. As such, fitness professionals can play an important role in helping their clients manage their diabetes.

Carbohydrate Metabolism During Exercise

❏ Overview

As discussed previously, the body can use carbohydrate, lipid, or protein for fuel during exercise. In a well-nourished state, protein contributes minimally as a fuel source (i.e., 5% of total). In reality, most of the fuel that the body needs comes from either carbohydrate or fat. Accordingly, the ratios of carbohydrate versus fat in fueling skeletal muscle are emphasized in the following sections of this chapter.

❏ Exercise Intensity

Table 5-1 shows that as exercise intensity increases, the body has a greater reliance on carbohydrate (CHO) for fuel. In Table 5-1, exercise intensity is gauged in terms of $\dot{V}O_{2max}$, which is the maximum rate at which the body can consume oxygen during exercise. The greater the percentage of $\dot{V}O_{2max}$, the greater the level of exercise intensity.

Intensity (I)	Energy Source
$I \leq 30\%$ $\dot{V}O_{2max}$	Primarily fat
$30\% \dot{V}O_{2max} < I \leq 50\% \dot{V}O_{2max}$	Fat > CHO
$50\% \dot{V}O_{2max} < I \leq 70\% \dot{V}O_{2max}$	CHO > Fat
$I > 70\% \dot{V}O_{2max}$	Primarily CHO

Table 5.1 Energy source relative to the level of exercise intensity

Obviously, as exercise intensity increases, adenosine triphosphate (ATP) demand increases. Which metabolic pathways can produce ATP quickly, with no need of oxygen to meet the elevated demand? One such pathway is the ATP-PC system. Because this system is very short-lasting, it is most relevant during explosive activities that last 10 seconds or less. The other system is glycolysis, which produces ATP at a relatively fast rate solely from the metabolism of carbohydrate. Viewing it from this perspective, it becomes apparent why carbohydrate is the primary source of fuel during high-intensity, short-term activities. Another reason that carbohydrates are used more readily than fats during high-intensity exercise is that an increased reliance on fast-twitch muscle fibers exists during such activity. These fibers have the essential machinery to support anaerobic glycolysis (i.e., more glycolytic enzymes and fewer mitochondrial and lipolytic enzymes). In addition, the hormonal profile observed during intense exercise, including increased levels of epinephrine, norepinephrine, and glucagon, and a decreased level of insulin, favors increased glycogen breakdown and glycolysis.

The problem with relying on glycolysis too heavily is that because it produces metabolic by-products that ultimately cause fatigue, glycolysis cannot continue indefinitely. Furthermore, since glycogen storage in the human body is limited, long-duration activities must have alternative fuel systems in order to continue unabated. Aerobic metabolism is a system that can continue for very long times with little accumulation of fatigue-inducing by-products. Immense quantities of ATP can be produced from the oxidation of fatty acids and to a lesser extent from the oxidation of glucose. Even though more ATP is generated from fatty acids in total, glucose breakdown provides more energy per liter of oxygen used. In an environment where oxygen is limited, such as during intense exercise, glucose is a more oxygen-efficient fuel. Oxidation of fat and carbohydrates to ATP is a relatively slow process that is not ideally suited for high-intensity activities. On the other hand, with appropriate training, the body's ability to oxidize substrates can be enhanced to enable an individual to work at higher intensity levels.

❑   Fat Burning

One popularly held view asserts that exercising at a low level of intensity for a long duration is necessary to maximize fat burning. Although it is true that at low-intensity exercise a greater percentage of energy is derived from fat than from carbohydrates, the total amount of calories burned during such activities is relatively low. In fact, individuals would be far better off exercising at a higher intensity level because their total energy expenditure and fat burning would actually be higher than at lower intensities, even though the percentage of fat calories burned would be lower.

Since glycogen storage in the human body is limited, long-duration activities must have alternative fuel systems in order to continue unabated.

If fitness professionals have healthy clients who are reasonably fit and want to maximize "fat-burning" in a short period of time, they should consider having those individuals exercise at higher intensities.

To better understand the aforementioned point, it would be helpful to compare two 30-minute workouts—one at low intensity and one at moderate intensity. During the low-intensity workout, an individual would burn 200 calories, of which 80%, or 160 calories, would be derived from fat. During the moderate-intensity workout, an individual would burn 400 calories, but only 50%, or 200 calories, would be from fat. Although the percentage of fat burned during the moderate-intensity activity would be lower, the total number of fat calories used would be greater. This trend extrapolates to high-intensity exercise as well, with even more benefits. All factors considered, high-intensity exercise tends to enhance fitness improvements more so than low-intensity training. In addition, high-intensity exercise, because it also metabolizes carbohydrates, causes some glycogen depletion. As such, post-exercise meals containing carbohydrate should be consumed to replenish the body's glycogen stores before any carbohydrate gets converted to triglyceride.

Given the aforementioned factors, if fitness professionals have healthy clients who are reasonably fit and want to maximize "fat-burning" in a short period of time, they should consider having those individuals exercise at higher intensities. For less-fit or less-motivated clients, fitness professionals have several options, including extending the length of the workout, while keeping the intensity level relatively low, to burn the same number of fat calories in a single exercise session.

Carbohydrate Needs

❑ Sedentary, Healthy Individuals

The adult DRI for carbohydrates is 45-65% of total daily calories. Expressing a person's daily carbohydrate needs numerically in the form of required carbohydrate calories that should be consumed may be somewhat confusing to many individuals. Some individuals seem to prefer to have a carbohydrate target value expressed in grams. The following example illustrates the conversion of a 2000 kcal per day diet that is 50% carbohydrate to daily carbohydrate grams:

- 2000 x 50% = 1000 carbohydrate kcal
- 1000 kcal ÷ 4 g/kcal = 250 g of carbohydrate per day (a carbohydrate has 4 kcal per gram)

1400 calorie diet
x 50%
700 ÷ 4g/cal
= 175g/day

Although the carbohydrate range of 45-65% is relatively broad, it meets the needs of most healthy individuals. Some individuals may be more compliant and feel healthier at the lower end of the range, while other people may do better at the upper end. As such, fitness professionals should not tell their clients specifically how much carbohydrate that they should eat. Rather, they should inform them of the DRI range and teach them how to choose foods that will help them consume the desired amount of that nutrient. It is important to keep in mind that the DRI range only applies to healthy individuals. For example, for an individual with a disease or medical condition, the DRIs may not be appropriate. In such a situation, the fitness professional should refer that individual to a registered dietitian.

❑ Active, Healthy Individuals

Physically active individuals usually need more carbohydrate than their sedentary counterparts due to their increased use of glycogen as fuel. Because the DRI range for carbohydrates encompasses the increased need of active individuals, it is likely that such people would want to consume carbohydrate at the higher end of the DRI range. Finding the right amount of carbohydrate within the range to match activity levels is a trial-and-error process. Most competitive athletes engage in this undertaking and get to know what works best for them. On the other hand, many physically active individuals, college athletes, and recreational athletes need more guidance in this area. It should be noted that all of the aforementioned recommendations concerning carbohydrate consumption are for healthy individuals. People with a medical condition may need alternate guidelines.

1400 x .65 =
910 ÷ 4 =
227.5g/day

❑ The Importance of Carbohydrate to Performance

It is critically important to maintain glycogen stores during endurance activity. Once glycogen stores become depleted, the body will simply slow down, as fat becomes the predominant source of fuel. It is only during the later stages of prolonged exercise that protein may contribute up to 15% of the expended energy. Maximizing glycogen stores before activity and maintaining blood glucose during activity are paramount to being successful during endurance activities. The next three sections present strategies that can help individuals achieve these two objectives.

Before Exercise

There are no magical foods for competition and sports; the issue is simply a matter of quantity and timing of eating. The underlying goal is to provide the body with glucose, without consuming so much food that it is uncomfortable or consuming so little food that hunger is triggered. Ideally, all carbohydrate consumed prior to exercise would be out of the stomach and in some stage of the absorptive process, whether it be circulating in the bloodstream, being taken up by cells, or crossing the intestinal wall. As the principles of digestion that were reviewed previously pointed out, liquids are digested faster than solids, and fiber slows the digestive process, which causes waste to remain in the colon longer. Although no DRIs exist for pre-exercise carbohydrate intake, most credible sources recommend 1-4.5 g of carbohydrate per kilogram of body weight, depending on the type of food and the time of the event. Individuals who want more detailed meal-timing protocols should seek guidance from a credentialed dietetics professional.

People who consume carbohydrate before exercise are often preoccupied with GI. As such, they worry about reactive hypoglycemia, which is a transient condition where an individual's blood glucose level temporarily drops below normal in response to carbohydrate intake. While low blood glucose can certainly affect performance, this condition is not overly common. If a person suffers from this condition, however, lower GI foods or combinations of foods may be helpful. Fitness professionals should refer any clients who have this condition to a registered dietitian.

There are no magical foods for competition and sports; the issue is simply a matter of quantity and timing of eating.

Ryan McVay

Almost all elite competitors know the precise schedule of when they need to consume carbohydrate during exercise and what works best for them.

During Exercise

Ingesting carbohydrates during exercise does not enhance an individual's performance during all types of physical activity. In fact, only high-intensity activities lasting 30 minutes or more, or continuous endurance or intermittent high-intensity endurance activities lasting 60-90 minutes or more may benefit from carbohydrate supplementation during exercise. Credible sources recommend that consuming 15-20 g of carbohydrate every 15-20 minutes is sufficient to meet the requirements of such activities. This amount translates to 1/2 to 3/4 cup of sports drink every 15-20 minutes. (Additional information on sports drinks is presented in the carbohydrate supplementation section of this chapter.) It is important to note that the aforementioned carbohydrate recommendation is merely a guideline and that in fact, individual needs may vary. Some individuals may do better with 1/4 cup of carbohydrate supplementation during exercise, while others may prefer a full cup every 15-20 minutes. In reality, almost all elite competitors know the precise schedule of when they need to consume carbohydrate during exercise and what works best for them. While the aforementioned guidelines are designed to serve as a useful starting point, if a fitness professional is working with someone who has a slightly different schedule, that person's individual needs and preferences should not be ignored.

Recovery from Exercise

The major carbohydrate-related consideration post-exercise, particularly if the activity was very long or intense, is to replenish glycogen stores. Glycogen stores can be replenished at approximately 5-7% per hour and can take 20 hours or longer to fully replete. Credible sources recommend that post-exercise intake equal 1.0-1.5 g of carbohydrate per kilogram of body weight within 15 to 30 minutes after activity. It appears that the timing of consumption is critical and that the 30-minute deadline should not be extended. An additional 1.0-1.5 g of carbohydrate per kilogram of body weight is recommended every two hours afterwards, until a total of 7-10 g per kilogram of body weight has been consumed. For example, the total post-exercise carbohydrate recommendation for an athlete who weighs 150 pounds (68 kg) is 476-680 g (68 x 7 and 68 x 10). Accordingly, an amount equal to 68-102 g carbohydrate should be eaten immediately after exercise and also at intervals two, four, six, eight, 10, and 12 hours post-exercise.

While this guideline is relatively simple, many factors are still being researched. For example, does the addition of protein to the carbohydrate further enhance glycogen resynthesis? In this regard, limited research exists to suggest that adding protein to carbohydrate during recovery enhances glycogen synthesis. More studies have been found that support the conclusion that carbohydrate intake is the important factor and that such consumption is independent of lipid or protein intake. It has been determined, however, that protein may play a significant role in post-exercise skeletal muscle protein synthesis—an issue that will be addressed in Chapter 7.

Another controversial topic concerns GI. One of the traditional ways of thinking involved recommending high-GI foods post-exercise. While this conclusion is certainly not a bad idea, newer research suggests that total amount of carbohydrate is more important than the GI. As such, it is probably more practical to recommend that physically active individuals consume foods that are familiar to them and well-liked.

It should be kept in mind that the aforementioned recovery guidelines apply to athletes and physically active individuals who significantly deplete their glycogen stores. In fact, a person exercising for 30 minutes at a low level of intensity does not need to follow any of the aforementioned guidelines presented for before, during, or after exercise. Fitness professionals may be working with overweight individuals who fit this exercise pattern who think that they need to drink a sports drink during or after exercise because of the marketing of these products. In reality, these products contain extra energy (and calories) that may not be needed by these individuals.

❑ Carbohydrate Loading

Carbohydrate loading is a technique that typically begins a week before an endurance event, with the expressed purpose of maximizing glycogen stores.

Research data suggest that when individuals deplete skeletal muscle and the liver of glycogen and then replenish, they can increase glycogen stores to two to three times their normal levels. The following four-point strategy is commonly used by athletes before an event. It is important to note that these are guidelines only and should not replace personalized strategies that have been developed by a credentialed dietetics professional.

- One week before an event, a long workout is performed, in an effort to deplete glycogen stores. For most people, depending on the intensity level of the session, this workout can take one to three hours.
- Moderate carbohydrate intake and a normal exercise routine are continued for the next three days.
- The routine is then reversed for the next three days. The carbohydrate-intake level is high, and the exercise duration and intensity level is gradually tapered until the day before the event, which should be rest.
- On day eight, the day of the event, the individual's glycogen stores will hopefully be maximized.

How is it possible to tell if this process is working? In a research-laboratory setting, skeletal muscle biopsies can be performed to measure glycogen content. Obviously, this approach is certainly not practical. A simple alternative is for individuals to weigh themselves daily. For each gram of glycogen that is stored, almost 3 g of water are stored with it. As glycogen is depleted in the first few days, body weight should decline; during the last few days during glycogen repletion, body weight should rise.

iStockphoto/Thinkstock

Research data suggest that when the individuals deplete skeletal muscle and the liver of glycogen and then replenish, they can increase glycogen stores to two to three times their normal levels.

Carbohydrate Supplementation

❑ Sports Drinks

A number of carbohydrate-supplementation products are on the market. As such, the sports drink is the "original" option in this regard, and one that remains very popular. Sports drinks generally contain approximately 14-15 g of carbohydrate per cup. They also contain electrolytes that mimic quantities lost in sweat. Sports drinks are available in many flavors, a factor that serves to heighten their popularity. Research suggests that if a person likes the taste of a beverage, that individual will drink more. Specialty sports-drink formulas that contain extra electrolytes for people who are heavy sweaters are also available on the market, as are products with concentrated forms of carbohydrate that are designed for very long events.

Two questions concerning sports drinks that often come up are the following:

- *Why choose a sports drink over juice or soda?* The answer to this question is simple and based on scientific evidence. A 6-8% carbohydrate solution is best for the maximal absorption of glucose. In contrast, soda, juice, and fruit-flavored punches generally have twice the amount of carbohydrate per unit volume. This feature actually hinders glucose absorption and may cause gastrointestinal distress. In addition, sports drinks contain multiple forms of carbohydrate, including glucose, sucrose, fructose, and glucose polymers. Research suggests that this formulation is best for maximizing glucose absorption.
- *Can a homemade sports drink be made?* While the answer is "yes," some issues exist. For example, research suggests that fructose alone may cause gastrointestinal distress during exercise. A person could dilute juice with water (a 1:1 ratio) and then add a pinch of salt (many juices naturally contain potassium). The problem with this step is that the electrolyte levels of the beverage may be inexact, and the carbohydrate type may not be ideal. Unless individuals are adamant about making their own beverage, the commercially available formulas are quite inexpensive and readily available. Furthermore, they are even less expensive in the powdered form.

Another point that fitness professionals who are working with an individual who is training for an event and likes consuming sports drinks should consider is to encourage that person to find out what sports-drink product is being supplied, if any, during the event. This factor can be extremely important for a competitor who hates a popular flavor of a sports drink. As such, a person who has an aversion to a particular flavor will likely decrease intake of that sports drink, a step that could diminish that individual's level of performance.

❑ Gels and Other Products

In addition to sports drinks, a number of products, such as gels, jelly beans, and gummy candies, that contain both carbohydrate and electrolytes are available on the market. These products generally contain 25-30 g of carbohydrate per packet. It is essential that individuals read these labels carefully, because some of these products may contain other unwanted ingredients, like caffeine or herbs. Among the benefits of these products is that they are small and portable. The primary thing that they lack is fluid. As such, it is still important to consume water if these products are taken before, during, or after exercise.

❏ Bars

Quite a few bars exist on the market. Content-wise, they range from being high in carbohydrate to high in protein. Although the carbohydrate in these bars can fuel movement, these bars are not practical, because of the inconvenience and discomfort associated with chewing them. Furthermore, they contain no fluid.

Many bars are marketed as "energy bars." All too often, the term "energy" is abused on products. Given that a kilocalorie (kcal) is a unit of energy, anything that contains calories could be viewed as an "energy" food. Many products that use this term imply that their product is special or that the item may contain stimulants such as caffeine. Regrettably, no regulations currently exist on the use of this term on food product labels. Accordingly, it is important for fitness professionals to have their clients scrutinize labels on these bars and make informed choices. For example, if a person is looking to ingest a snack of 25-30 g of carbohydrate, does that individual need a specialized energy bar marketed for athletes or can that person get the same carbohydrate benefits from a common, inexpensive cereal bar? In reality, many of the "supermarket variety" bars use all-natural ingredients with no preservatives, and at a much lower cost than sports bars.

When looking for a high-quality bar, the most appropriate choice is one that contains at least 2 g each of fiber and protein, has less than 1 g of saturated/trans fat combined, and is made from whole grain. In fact, whole grain should be listed first on the ingredient's label. Individuals who are looking for bars that are relatively high in fiber have many options, including a number of bars that each contain more than 10 g of fiber.

Summary

Glucose, the usable form of carbohydrate in the body, is an important fuel source for many organs, including skeletal muscle. A person's dietary carbohydrate needs will vary depending on the level of physical activity. For athletes and physically active individuals, it is important to eat enough carbohydrate to sustain activity demands, and to take in additional carbohydrate before, during, and after exercise in order to maintain and replenish glycogen stores. Many food sources are rich in carbohydrate. In addition, several types of carbohydrate-containing products are available for use during athletic events.

One of the basic goals of fitness professionals should be to teach their clients about the relationship between carbohydrate and performance. This effort by fitness professionals to inform their clients should include a discussion of the concepts of exercise intensity, carbohydrate digestion and metabolism, meal timing, and glycogen repletion. It is also important to keep in mind that while fitness professionals can provide their healthy clients with the appropriate guidelines concerning the consumption of carbohydrates, specific meal-planning should only be undertaken by a registered dietitian.

6

Lipids

Lipid Classification

Lipids contain the following three elements—carbon, hydrogen, and oxygen. Each gram of lipid contains nine calories of energy. A primary function of lipids is fuel, but they are also helpful with insulation, protection, transportation, and adding flavor and texture to foods. The form of lipid most common in the American diet and the variety stored in the human body is called a triglyceride (TG). A TG contains three fatty acids, which are composed of a long chain of carbon and hydrogen atoms bound together, connected to a small carbon-containing molecule called glycerol.

Lipids can be classified into fats and oils. Fats are usually solid at room temperature, while oils are liquids. Fats can be further classified by their degree of saturation. Saturated fats are those fats whose carbon atoms are bound to as many hydrogen atoms as chemically possible. Because saturated fatty acids are straight in shape, these molecules are tightly attracted to each other. It requires a lot of energy to separate them, which is why saturated fats tend to be solid at room temperature. Unsaturated fats, which include monounsaturated and polyunsaturated varieties, on the other hand, do not have the maximum number of hydrogen atoms attached to every carbon atom. Wherever a hydrogen atom is missing, a double-bond between two carbon atoms is in its place. Unsaturated fatty acids are not as strongly attracted to one another as are saturated fatty acids, because every double-bond creates a kink in the shape of the molecule. As a result, these fats tend to be liquid at room temperature. Monounsaturated fats, such as olive oil and canola oil, have only one double-bond, while polyunsaturated fats, including most vegetable oils, have more than one-double bond. Polyunsaturated fatty acids can be further categorized as either omega-6 or omega-3, depending on where the double bonds are located on the fatty acid. Both omega-6 and omega-3 fatty acids are essential, which means that they cannot be synthesized by the human body and must be consumed in the diet. Due to the high intake of fats in the American diet, essential fatty acid deficiencies are not common. However, the ratio of these fatty acids in the typical diet is not ideal. Omega-6 fatty acids, which are found in many vegetable oils, are often consumed in abundance, while omega-3 fatty acids are more limited. Common sources of omega-3 fatty acids include fatty fish, flax seed, and certain nuts (e.g., walnuts and almonds).

Considerable attention has been given to the role of trans fatty acids in the development of abnormal blood lipids and heart disease. Trans fat is the common name for a type of unsaturated fat that has been shown to be decidedly unhealthy. For example, research has shown that trans fats raise "bad" (low-density lipoprotein, or LDL) cholesterol levels and lower "good" (high-density lipoprotein, or HDL) cholesterol levels. As such, consuming trans fats will increase an individual's risk of developing both heart disease and type 2 diabetes, as well as suffering a stroke.

Trans fats can be found in many foods, including stick margarines and shortenings used in baking and frying foods (e.g., lard). A number of years ago, lard (animal fat) was commonly used to bake and fry foods. A solid substance at room temperature, lard gives flavor to food and provides a desirable texture. Over time, it developed the reputation of being bad for health. While an individual who is attempting to bake something could replace the called-for amount of animal fat with vegetable oil, anyone who has ever tried to bake pie crust or chocolate chip cookies with vegetable oil knows that the taste and texture would just not be right.

Trans fat is the common name for a type of unsaturated fat that has been shown to be decidedly unhealthy.

Food manufacturers attempted to solve this problem by developing a vegetable-based product that tastes and behaves like animal fat, but without the unhealthy side effects, or so they believed. In fact, artificially adding hydrogen molecules to polyunsaturated vegetable oil does make them more "fat-like." They become solid at room temperature, prevent rancidity, and are ideal for baking and frying. The resultant problem, however, is that the hydrogenation process places hydrogen atoms on opposite sides of the double bonds, or in the "trans" location. Because trans fatty acids are straight—with no kinks—they resemble saturated fatty acids, even though they are still unsaturated. While this solid, vegetable-based compound has great cooking properties, it possesses the unhealthful side effects of saturated fats, such as elevated lipids and cholesterol, which results in a greater risk of heart disease.

Digestion and Metabolism of Lipids

The primary site of lipid digestion is within the small intestine. Lipids are digested best with the help of a compound called bile, which is an emulsifying compound made by the liver and stored in the gallbladder. The presence of fat in the small intestine stimulates the release of bile, which breaks the large lipid globules into smaller units, thereby increasing the surface area upon which lipolytic enzymes can act. Pancreatic lipase is the enzyme that breaks down TG into its component fatty acids and glycerol, which then cross the intestinal wall. Since lipids are not water soluble, they cannot travel in the bloodstream by themselves. Instead, they must be transported inside vehicles that are water-soluble, namely lipoproteins.

Lipoproteins are predominantly lipid on the inside and protein on the outside. A chylomicron is a lipoprotein produced in the intestinal wall that carries absorbed dietary lipids and cholesterol through the lymphatic system to the bloodstream. The lipid located in chylomicrons has two fates. It is either delivered to active tissues and used as fuel or stored in adipose tissue as fat.

Most individuals who exercise have likely heard of HDL and LDL. These lipoproteins are produced when the liver converts excess dietary carbohydrate, lipids, and protein into lipoproteins and releases them into the bloodstream so that they can be used by body cells. The relative amount of lipid in the lipoprotein determines whether it is categorized as low or high density. Since lipid is less dense than protein, an LDL has more lipids than an HDL. Normally, LDLs are taken up by the liver and recycled back into the bloodstream as very low-density lipoproteins (VLDL), which target active cells and adipose tissue to unload their lipids. The uptake of LDL by the liver may be interfered with either by the consumption of saturated fat or trans fat or by the condition of obesity. Such interference contributes to elevated LDL levels in the blood. Over time, LDLs begin to degrade and release their lipids, including cholesterol, into the blood. Circulating cholesterol has been implicated as one of the major contributors to the development of arterial plaques and subsequent atherosclerosis. As a result, even though LDL is actually a lipoprotein, it is often called the "bad cholesterol" by the general public.

HDLs are important because these lipoproteins help to keep levels of total serum cholesterol within a normal range. HDL picks up cholesterol from arterial plaques and delivers it to tissues that can use it to make necessary compounds or send it back to the liver to make bile. This function is why HDL is often called the "good cholesterol," even though the characterization is not accurate.

Eising

HDLs are important because these lipoproteins help to keep levels of total serum cholesterol within a normal range.

Lipids and Health

The number one cause of death in the United Sates is cardiovascular disease (CVD). Although CVD has a number of risk factors, two of the controllable ones are dietary intake and appropriate levels of physical activity. Because diets that are high in saturated and trans fats tend to increase levels of total and LDL cholesterol, they also elevate the risk of atherogenesis. One of the steps in the formation of atherogenic plaques is the oxidation of the LDL molecule. For health reasons, it is important to keep this oxidation under control. In that regard, it is believed that a diet rich in antioxidants and low in saturated and trans fats may be helpful. Antioxidant nutrients are abundant in fruits and vegetables and are present in whole grains. Unfortunately, taking antioxidants in a supplemental "pill" form may not have the same benefits.

Some of the larger studies conducted do not necessarily support supplementation with antioxidants. Data from the Physicians' Health Study found no decrease in the risk of cancer, heart disease, or diabetes with 12 years of beta-carotene supplementation in 22,000 men. In the Heart Protection Study, 20,000 participants experienced no difference in heart attack rates after five years of supplementation with vitamin E, vitamin C, and beta-carotene (Heart Protection Study Collaborative Group, 2002). Data from the Women's Health Study indicate that taking vitamin E for 10 years had no effect in heart disease, stroke, or cancer rates for healthy female professionals. Conclusions from studies like these do not signify that antioxidants are unimportant for preventative health. However, until more research is completed, it is prudent to refrain from recommending supplementation for all individuals, or, more importantly, imply that supplementation is somehow a guarantee of protection. On the other hand, it is reasonable to discuss the health benefits of the antioxidants found in foods and encourage consumption of these foods with those individuals interested in supplementation.

The relationship between dietary fat and cancer is not as clear as the relationship that dietary fat has with CVD. Despite the numerous studies published, no definitive answer exists. While a positive relationship may exist between cancer risk and consuming a diet high in fat and low in plant foods, the mechanisms of how fat consumption contributes to the development of cancer are unclear.

Omega-3 fatty acids are also believed to have an impact on health. In reality, the American diet is generally low in omega-3 fatty acids. This factor is particularly relevant when newer data that suggests that atherosclerosis and CVD are partially an inflammatory process is considered. Since omega-3 fatty acids may help control this inflammation, they may help prevent the development of both atherogenesis and CVD. Daily recommendations for the consumption of omega-3 fatty acids for optimal health are listed in the next section.

Quite a bit of data exists to support consuming a Mediterranean-style diet for maintaining optimal lipid profiles.

Dietary Needs

The DRI for total fat is 20-35% of total daily calories. Separate DRIs have been developed for omega-6 fatty acids and omega-3 fatty acids by gender and life stage (refer to Appendix C2). The adult DRI for omega-6 fatty acids and omega-3 fatty acids is 5-10% of daily energy needs and 0.6-1.2% of daily energy needs, respectively. Some individuals maintain a healthy lipid profile by adhering to the guidelines for the lower end of the total fat spectrum, while others fare better by following the suggested parameters for the higher end. It should be noted that people who select the upper end of the DRI range should be choosing healthy fats, not saturated or trans fats.

Quite a bit of data exists to support consuming a Mediterranean-style diet for maintaining optimal lipid profiles. While this diet is high in total fat, the fat intake tends to be primarily from healthy sources, such as fish and olive oil. The diet also includes fruits, vegetables, and whole grains. There is not a DRI for saturated or trans fats, since they are not required in the diet.

The DRI for lipids applies to both sedentary and physically active individuals. Competitive endurance athletes will often end up at the lower end of the range, due to their increased requirement for carbohydrate and protein. While research data are extremely limited, evidence exists to suggest that chronic intake of fat below 20% of total calories may result in a reduced level of testosterone production in men. It is important to keep in mind that these data cannot be used to draw an absolute conclusion. Furthermore, similar data in women have not been published.

Due to the considerable amount of information that exists regarding the health benefits of omega-3 fatty acids, a number people are turning to meals containing fish. The types of fish rich in omega-3 fatty acids include salmon, tuna, sardines, anchovies, striped bass, catfish, herring, mackerel, trout, halibut, mussels, crab, and shrimp. Since information on omega-3 fatty acids is not currently required to be noted on a food label, the most practical advice to give individuals who would like to eat more omega-3 fatty acids is to consume fish with darker flesh. Consuming too much fish, however, can lead to toxic metal poisoning, particularly mercury poisoning. The current recommendation for fish consumption is to limit it to 12 ounces per week.

Individuals who prefer an alternate source of omega-3 fatty acids have several options, including flaxseed, flaxseed oil, or nuts, particularly almonds and walnuts. If flaxseeds are to be consumed, they must be ground, since the whole seed is not digestible. In addition, the ground seeds should be kept in a freezer to preserve their freshness. Flaxseed and flaxseed oil often turn rancid very quickly.

Chris Clinton

Trained individuals can use more fat for fuel than untrained persons.

Lipid Metabolism During Exercise

The TG stored in adipose tissue is a basic source of fuel during exercise. The other lipid storage compartment that plays a role in providing fuel during exercise is intra-muscular triglyceride (IMTG). As the intensity level of the exercise bout increases, the body relies more on IMTG to contribute to the total portion of the fuel that is supplied by fat. In fact, individuals who are trained have a larger reserve of IMTG than untrained individuals, which makes sense, because IMTG is more rapidly available due to its location than adipose tissue TG. The adipose tissue TG must be first broken down and transported to the skeletal muscle before it can be used. In addition to having a greater quantity of IMTG, a trained individual also has the ability to use more fat for fuel. As a result, this person can spare glycogen better than an untrained person.

Fat Loading and Performance

Since trained individuals can use more fat for fuel than untrained persons, the idea of increasing a person's consumption level of fat to improve their exercise performance level has been advanced in some quarters. In that regard, a few studies have examined the concept of employing fat-loading to enhance an individual's performance level during physical activity. The data, however, show that high-fat diets do not result in a performance benefit and, in fact, may be undesirable from a palatability and long-term health standpoint.

Summary

Several types of lipids exist in the diet, some of which are better for a person's health than others. While the body has minimal required levels of essential fatty acids, the overconsumption of other types of fatty acids can increase an individual's risk of developing cardiovascular disease. Fat is an important fuel source for the body, especially during low-intensity or prolonged exercise. While athletes tend to experience some metabolic adaptations to fat metabolism, the dietary recommendations for these individuals do not differ from the general population.

7

Protein

Protein Classification

Protein contains the following four elements: carbon, hydrogen, oxygen, and nitrogen. Protein has many functions and can be categorized as structural or regulatory. Examples of structural proteins include skin, cell membranes, and bone tissue. Regulatory proteins include enzymes, transport proteins (e.g., lipoproteins, hemoglobin), defense proteins (e.g., antibodies), contractile proteins (e.g., actin and myosin of skeletal muscle), hormones, protein pumps, and serum protein to help maintain fluid and electrolyte balance.

*

The smallest unit of a protein is called an amino acid. Two amino acids joined together form a dipeptide; three form a tripeptide; and many joined together form a polypeptide. One or more folded polypeptide chains form a protein molecule.

Protein Quality

Proteins in the human body are composed of 20 different amino acids. The nine essential amino acids (histidine, isoleucine, leucine, lysine, methionine, phenylalanine, threonine, tryptophan, and valine) are ones the body cannot make and are required in the diet. The 11 nonessential amino acids (alanine, arginine, asparagine, aspartic acid, cysteine, glutamic acid, glutamine, glycine, proline, serine, and tyrosine) can be synthesized in the body and, therefore, are not required in the diet.

Complete proteins contain all of the essential amino acids in one product, while incomplete proteins lack at least one. A good rule of thumb: if a product is animal flesh or comes from an animal, then it is a complete protein. Soy protein, from a plant, is one of the exceptions to the rule. Soy does contain all the essential amino acids, while most other plants lack at least one of the

Complete proteins contain all of the essential amino acids in one product, while incomplete proteins lack at least one.

essential amino acids and are incomplete proteins. Vegans, who choose not to consume any animal products, may have concerns that their protein needs are not met. Many incomplete proteins, when combined together, provide all of the essential amino acids. For example, rice and beans or peanut butter and bread are great complementary proteins. It is important for vegans to have some variety in the diet if they are relying on complementary proteins, but protein needs can be met with careful planning. Vegans should also be mindful of the following nutrients: riboflavin, vitamin B12, calcium, vitamin D (if sun exposure is limited), iron, and zinc. These nutrients can be consumed in fortified foods or in a supplemental form if necessary.

❑ Protein Digestibility-Corrected Amino Acid Score (PDCAAS)

The Protein Digestibility-Corrected Amino Acid Score (PDCAAS) is the Food and Drug Administration's official method for determining protein quality, accounting for both amino acid composition and digestibility. In general, protein from animal sources are more than 90% digestible; beans and legumes are approximately 80% digestible; and other grains and vegetables are less digestible overall but can range from 60-90%. The percent Daily Value (%DV) on a Nutrition Facts Label may differ for the same quantity of different protein sources since the PDCAAS is used. For example, both 1 ounce of meat and one-half cup of cooked beans contain approximately 7 g of protein. However, the foods would contribute differently to total amino acid needs and, therefore, the %DV would be different on the label.

❑ Biological Value

The term biological value (BV) is often used by supplement manufacturers to promote their product as being superior to another product or to foods. BV compares the amount of nitrogen absorbed from the diet to the amount retained in the body for maintenance and growth. Numeric values are available for many foods, but it is much more practical for a client to list or group those foods that have a high BV. For example, most animal foods have a similar value and are considered high BV protein sources.

Digestion and Metabolism of Protein

Protein digestion begins in the stomach with the aid of pepsin. However, the primary site of protein digestion is the small intestine, where enzymes called proteases digest the proteins into smaller units for absorption. Unlike dietary carbohydrates that must be broken down to the smallest unit (monosaccharides), proteins can be absorbed as tripeptides, dipeptides, and free amino acids. Each of these smaller units has its own transporter site to cross the intestinal wall, similar to having three different doorways for entry. Many supplement manufacturers claim that free amino acids are superior because they are already broken down from the joined amino acids. However, the small intestine is quite capable of absorbing the di- and tripeptides, as well as free amino acids. Additionally, supplemental free amino acids tend to be quite expensive when compared to the same quantity available in foods. Once the amino acids are absorbed, they travel to the liver via the hepatic portal vein.

When the amino acids resulting from protein digestion reach the liver, one of the following will occur:

- The nitrogen from the amino acids can be used to synthesize nonprotein, nitrogenous compounds like creatine.
- The amino acids can be used to synthesize proteins.
- The amino acids can be used to synthesize nonessential amino acids.
- Some amino acids can be used to make glucose.
- The amino acids can be used for adenosine triphosphate (ATP) synthesis (under normal conditions, protein contributes approximately only 5% towards total energy needs).

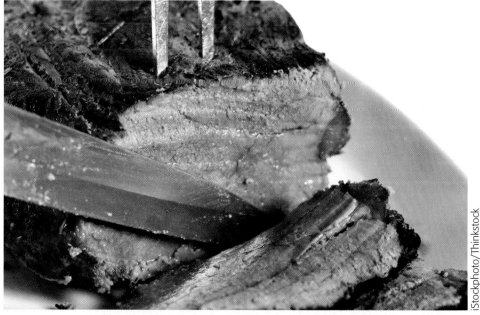

iStockphoto/Thinkstock

Unlike dietary carbohydrates that must be broken down to the smallest unit (monosaccharides), proteins can be absorbed as tripeptides, dipeptides, and free amino acids.

Dietary fats have two fates: to be used for fuel or stored in adipose tissue (or intramuscular triglyceride).

If the prior needs are met, and extra amino acids are present, the liver can take the carbon skeleton from an amino acid, synthesize a fatty acid, and store it in the adipose tissue. When glucose or fatty acids are formed from carbon skeletons of the amino acid, or if the carbon skeleton is used for ATP synthesis, the nitrogen is removed, used to make urea by the liver, and then the urea is excreted by the kidney.

One of the metabolic fates of some amino acids is the ability to make glucose from glucogenic amino acids. The body will prioritize organ function and the brain needs glucose to function. If a person is starving, glucose must always be maintained for the brain and can be made from the breakdown of skeletal muscle. One reason for the catabolism of skeletal muscle in individuals who are starving is that glucose cannot be made from a fatty acid (only a minimal amount can be made from the glycerol backbone of the triglyceride molecule).

Dietary fats have two fates: to be used for fuel or stored in adipose tissue (or intramuscular triglyceride). Glucose, from the ingestion of dietary carbohydrate, has three fates: to be used for fuel, stored as glycogen, or converted to fatty acids and stored in the adipose tissue. The body does not store protein as it does fats and carbohydrates; there is no equivalent to the glycogen stored in the muscle and liver or to the triglyceride stored in the adipose tissue. Skeletal muscle tissue is broken down in times of starvation but should not be considered the storage tank of smaller protein units or amino acids.

Dietary Needs

Dietary protein needs can be determined in the laboratory by a couple of methods. Measuring nitrogen balance is a classical method for precisely determining protein needs. Determining nitrogen needs is all that is required since protein is 16% nitrogen and is the only macronutrient that contains nitrogen. When the body is in negative nitrogen balance, it is in a catabolic state where amino acids are being oxidized. In contrast, when nitrogen balance is positive, the body is in an anabolic state, and amino acids are being incorporated into proteins. When the body is in nitrogen balance (nitrogen intake equals the nitrogen losses in the urine and feces), the protein requirements for the body are being met. This methodology requires that every drop of food intake be controlled and all excrements are collected. A sophisticated laboratory is needed where subjects reside in the facility and extensive equipment is available to analyze the nitrogen content of the food and bodily excretions.

Another newer method involves the use of radioisotopes to measure skeletal muscle protein synthesis and breakdown. With this methodology, the carbon molecules in an amino acid (most commonly leucine) are labeled or tagged with radiation to be traced through metabolic processes in the body. The amount of protein that is needed to reach a plateau in skeletal muscle protein synthesis is considered the protein requirement for the body.

❑ Sedentary, Healthy Individuals

The DRI for daily dietary protein in adults 19-50 years old is 10-35% of total calories or 0.8 grams per kilogram (g/kg) of body weight. See the DRI tables in Appendix C2 for protein needs listed by gender and life stage.

❑ Physically Active Individuals and Athletes

Protein requirements are different for highly active individuals, as the DRI of 0.8 g/kg will likely not be enough to maintain nitrogen balance. Based on the current available research data, endurance athletes need between 1.1 and 1.5 g/kg per day and resistance-trained athletes need between 1.5 and 2.0 g/kg per day. The increased protein needs can be met with food, with no need for supplementation. Though many active individuals and athletes know they need more protein than their sedentary counterparts, some may consume several grams per kilogram of body weight per day. Can the body use all of this protein? The answer appears to be no. Studies measuring skeletal muscle protein synthesis find that protein synthesis plateaus at a protein intake of 2.0-2.4 g/kg, meaning that protein intakes higher than this value are not being used to build muscle.

Protein Metabolism During Exercise

As mentioned in earlier sections, most of the fuel used during exercise comes from a combination of carbohydrate and fat, while only about 5% of the generated ATP comes from protein. An exception to this rule is at the later stages of prolonged endurance exercise, where protein can contribute up to 15% towards ATP production. The physiological explanation for this is simple: blood glucose must be maintained. As glycogen stores are depleted, blood glucose levels are in jeopardy. Since the body cannot make glucose from a fatty acid molecule, it must turn to protein for the synthesis of glucose.

Resistance training also results in a metabolic change in protein metabolism. During a resistance-training session, protein breakdown is generally occurring. Postexercise, a marked increase in protein synthesis occurs such that the net protein balance is positive, which is necessary to build skeletal muscle. In order to promote this positive protein synthesis, adequate levels of both energy and protein need to be consumed. A question that remains to be answered is when this increase in protein synthesis is seen postexercise. Unfortunately, the data are very limited because the methodology for determining protein balance is fairly new, quite expensive, and few laboratories have the ability to perform this research. At this point, the data suggest that increased protein synthesis occurs anywhere between immediately after exercise and up to 48 hours postexercise. As research progresses, hopefully a more concrete answer will become available to establish more detailed protein-consumption guidelines.

Jupiterimages

Most of the fuel used during exercise comes from a combination of carbohydrate and fat, while only about 5% of the generated ATP comes from protein.

Protein Intake and Supplementation

❑ Types of Protein Supplements

One of the most popular forms of supplemental protein is whey protein. When milk curdles, the solid curds contain the protein casein, while the liquid portion contains the protein whey. Whey contains a high concentration of branched-chain amino acids (isoleucine, leucine, and valine), which play an important role in exercise metabolism and protein synthesis. Supplemental whey protein comes in different varieties:

- Whey protein concentrates can range in protein content, but generally contain approximately 80% amino acids. They also contain lactose, fat, and minerals.
- Whey protein isolates are the purest form of whey protein and usually contain 90-95% amino acids with little or no lactose and fat. They tend to be more expensive than whey protein concentrates.
- Hydrolyzed whey protein is broken down to peptides and therefore may reduce the potential for an allergic reaction in individuals sensitive to milk protein. It is commonly used in infant formulas and some sports drinks.

Another type of protein supplement is soy protein, which tends to be more commonly used by women. Soy protein supplementation should be considered with caution in some situations. This high-quality plant protein contains isoflavones, or plant forms of estrogens. Many breast tumors appear to be sensitive to estrogen and will grow when exposed to this hormone. The research data on soy consumption and breast cancer is unclear. Some studies suggest that the phytoestrogens in soy may bind to breast tumors and prevent endogenous estrogen from binding, thereby reducing the risk of tumor growth. Other studies suggest that the phytoestrogens in soy may bind to a breast tumor, behave like estrogen, and promote tumor growth. Until research data on this topic are clearer, it is best not to excessively supplement with soy if there is a strong family history of breast cancer or if the disease is present. This does not mean all soy foods should be avoided, but clients should not consume them in excess, especially in the supplemental form.

Strong data exists to suggest a relationship between soy protein intake and cardiovascular disease (CVD) and, in fact, the FDA has approved a health claim for this relationship (see Chapter 2 or visit www.fda.gov for more information). The data suggest that *replacing* 25 g per day of animal protein with soy protein may reduce the risk of CVD. This statement appears on the label of food products containing soy. Notice the statement says to *replace* the animal protein with soy protein. This statement does not mean an individual should continue to consume a diet high in saturated and trans fats and then supplement with soy to get the protective effects.

Many male body builders will avoid soy protein because of the fear of the phytoestrogens and the potential side effects, such as growth of breast tissue.

Only one study in this area has been published, and it reported that 12 weeks of soy consumption in men did not reduce testosterone levels or inhibit lean body mass changes. More data are needed to confirm these findings, but consuming soy in modest amounts will likely not be problematic in altering hormone production.

❑ Before and During Exercise

Based on the abundant research data, supplementing with carbohydrate before, during, and after exercise improves endurance performance. Since resistance training causes a disruption in protein balance, with a goal of increasing muscle growth, does supplementation with protein aid in this process? Unfortunately, not nearly as much research data is available examining this question as is available investigating carbohydrate intake. However, the available data can be shared with clients to make the best of their training.

It appears that when carbohydrate alone or in combination with protein is ingested postexercise, an insulin response occurs. Insulin is an anabolic hormone that plays a role in protein synthesis. It is not clear if carbohydrate and protein intake should be staggered or combined for maximal skeletal muscle protein synthesis. More research is needed on this topic.

Strong evidence exists for the daily protein needs to maintain nitrogen balance in various endurance and resistance-trained athletes. This question remains: how is the protein intake distributed over the day to maximize protein synthesis? Is it better to spread protein throughout the day or eat larger meals? Only a couple of studies have examined spaced versus single-dose protein feeding in older and younger women, and with conflicting results. Furthermore, these studies did not compare pre- versus post-training, and the results cannot be used to make absolute conclusions.

Many of the earlier studies on protein supplementation specifically examined the effect of protein intake postexercise on skeletal muscle protein synthesis. Though studies are limited, it has been suggested that as little as 6 g of protein ingested an hour or two postexercise enhances protein synthesis, compared to no protein intake after the workout. More studies are needed before concrete conclusions can be made, but based on the available evidence it would be wise to eat protein-rich foods postexercise.

What about pre-exercise protein consumption? There are even fewer research studies examining this question. A couple of studies came to the same conclusion: as little as 6-10 g of protein ingested before a resistance-training workout resulted in greater protein synthesis compared to protein ingested postexercise. Other studies found no difference in protein synthesis when protein was consumed before versus after exercise. From a physiological standpoint, this seems logical. It takes a few hours or more to digest food, depending on the meal size and nutrient composition. If protein synthesis increases postexercise, having some amino acids readily available for the process will optimize the outcome. More data are needed before concrete recommendations can be made. However, it cannot hurt to consume a protein-rich snack prior to a resistance-training workout. 6-10 g of protein can be found in a yogurt, an ounce of meat or cheese, or a glass of milk.

Another common question: what is the best form of protein to maximize skeletal muscle protein synthesis? This question does not have a clear answer. While a few studies have been done on this topic, the answer is not conclusive. A recent study examined the effects of whey protein versus casein on body composition in recreational body builders. This study did suggest that whey protein was better for reducing fat mass and increasing strength; however, this is only one study. More research of this nature needs to be completed before any conclusions can be made. Two other recently published studies examined the effects of milk versus soy supplementation during a period of resistance training. The results of both studies suggest that milk protein was superior; one study reported increased skeletal muscle hypertrophy, while the other reported a greater fat-mass loss. Though more research is needed, it is encouraging to see research supporting the consumption of a simple, inexpensive, and readily available product such as milk.

A final question that fitness professionals may encounter is about maximal dosing of a protein supplement. What is the optimal amount of protein in a single dose? This question may seem simple, yet few studies have been conducted examining this issue. An earlier study showed that larger amounts of protein (i.e., 40 g) taken postexercise may exceed the maximal effective dose. A more recent study examined doses of 0, 5, 10, 20, and 40 g of protein and reported that 20 g of egg protein isolate was the maximal dose to stimulate skeletal muscle protein synthesis without drastically increasing amino acid oxidation (an indication that the protein is being wasted).

❑   Recovery From Exercise

Much research data support the use of carbohydrate intake postexercise to replenish glycogen stores. In general, the research data do not support the need for protein ingestion postexercise in order to maximize glycogen replenishment. However, protein intake postexercise may play a significant role in maximizing skeletal muscle protein synthesis, and small quantities are likely to be effective. From this standpoint, it is probably a good idea to include some protein in the postworkout meal. The common recommended ratio of carbohydrate:protein is 4:1. Specialized products are on the market that have this perfect ratio in one product, but keep in mind that the postexercise meal can be in the form of food. Research supports the fact that a glass of chocolate milk is an excellent recovery beverage. Many protein supplement powders promote their isoleucine and leucine content (both are branched-chain amino acids that play a role in protein synthesis). A 16-ounce glass of chocolate milk, 6 ounces of canned tuna, or one cup of cottage cheese has similar amounts of these "recovery" amino acids. In addition, the cost per gram of protein is much

Daily protein needs are greater for active individuals and athletes than for sedentary individuals; however, these increased needs can be met with food.

Jupiterimages

less with the food products than with the supplement. The supplement, however, does offer the convenience of being portable with no refrigeration required.

Summary

Protein has several functions in the body. Protein quality varies from different food sources, with the highest quality generally coming from animal products. Daily protein needs are greater for active individuals and athletes than for sedentary individuals; however, these increased needs can be met with food. While these daily protein needs are based on solid research data, there is not an abundant amount of research available to provide specific guidelines for protein intake before, during, or after resistance training to optimize protein synthesis. Limited data do suggest that small amounts of protein consumed before and after a resistance-training workout may be beneficial for maximizing skeletal muscle protein synthesis.

8

Vitamins and Minerals

Vitamins and minerals that are needed in the body in small quantities are classified as micronutrients. Vitamins can also be classified as fat-soluble or water-soluble. The fat-soluble vitamins—Vitamins A, D, E, and K—require dietary fat for absorption and are stored in adipose tissue. Water-soluble vitamins are not stored in the body, are depleted more rapidly, and, therefore, need to be consumed regularly. A common myth is that no toxic effects can occur from water-soluble vitamins since they are excreted rather than stored. While, some water-soluble vitamins are not toxic, others are. The vitamins that have an established Tolerable Upper Intake Level (UL) (defined in Chapter 2) have potential side effects.

Though each micronutrient has a specific function, some act as coenzymes in metabolic reactions. Despite a popular belief that vitamins provide "energy," they are not energy nutrients, as they do not contain calories. Many vitamins play an important role in the energy systems (discussed in Chapter 3), but taking quantities in excess of physiological needs will not increase ATP production. However, true vitamin deficiency may result in impaired energy metabolism and, hence, impaired performance.

Dietary Reference Intakes

As mentioned in Chapter 2, the Dietary Reference Intakes (DRIs) are published by the National Academy of Sciences (www.nationalacademies.org). The reports can also be accessed via the USDA website (www.usda.gov). A copy of the DRIs is located in Appendix C2 of this book.

The DRIs are guidelines designed to be used as goals for almost all healthy individuals (97-98%). For those who are free from disease and other medical conditions, the DRIs can be used as a goal for individual intake. The DRIs, categorized by gender and life stages, are quite easy to use. Keep copies handy to share with interested clients. Before discussing these guidelines with clients, it is a good idea to be familiar with the terms mentioned in the footnotes of the document.

However, in the DRIs, no category exists for athletes. Though research data on micronutrient requirements for athletes are not as abundant as for the general population, it appears that most of the DRIs are appropriate for healthy athletes and healthy active individuals. A few of the micronutrients may be of concern for athletes and are discussed in the following sections. For those who have a disease or medical condition, the DRIs should not be presented as a guide, and a registered dietitian should be consulted.

Vitamin and Mineral Supplements

Clients will likely ask if they should take a multivitamin/mineral (MVM) supplement or individual micronutrient supplements. Some people may believe that adding a MVM is a helpful "insurance policy" that cannot be harmful. As mentioned in Chapter 2, caution should be used when recommending supplements to clients. First, all of the issues with current supplement regulation need to be discussed. Can the claims and ingredient quantities listed on the label be believed? It is questionable if 500% or 1,000% of the Daily Value (DV) is needed for the body. Greater than 100% of the DV may be toxic, so individuals should refer to the UL table of the DRIs. It is important to keep in mind that people may be consuming a MVM in addition to fortified energy bars, vitamin waters, fitness waters, and fortified foods such as soy milk or orange juice. A formal nutrition assessment performed by a registered dietitian may be warranted for those who use these products regularly.

It is appropriate to share the research data and then let the individual make the decision to supplement. However, the individual who is deciding whether or not to supplement should also be educated about the current UL for each of the nutrients. It should be stressed that the phrase "not determinable" on the UL tables means that available data are limited and guidelines cannot be set regarding the largest quantities that are safe. Food should be the only source of these nutrients. For those nutrients that do have a UL listed, it can be very difficult to reach that level solely with food intake. It is the excessive nutrient intake from supplements and fortified foods that may cause problems.

If an individual eats well, but chooses to take a MVM to ensure nutrient adequacy, a product with no nutrients listed at more than 100% of the DV should be chosen. Even if someone does eat well and consumes 100% of the DV, they are unlikely to approach the UL. Some nutrients, for example calcium, may be listed on the supplement's label at lower than 100% of the DV because if each serving contained the full amount, the tablet would be too large to ingest. A DV lower than 100% does not imply that the supplement is inadequate.

State statutes should be consulted before a discussion on the use of a MVM supplement. In some states, performing a nutrition assessment and then following it by recommending specific quantities of foods or supplements may be in violation of the law. However, it is appropriate that clients are educated with general, nonmedical nutrition information regarding supplement regulation and good-to-excellent food sources of nutrients.

Vitamins and Minerals That May Need Attention in Athletes

❑ B-Vitamins

Some data suggest that thiamin needs may be slightly greater in athletes. Thiamin is abundant in foods made with flour, corn, and whole-grain breads and cereals and is also available in many processed food products that have been enriched. Since most athletes and active individuals need more calories than sedentary individuals, the slightly greater thiamin need can be met by the increased food intake that is required to meet the demands of activity.

❑ Antioxidants

A topic currently being researched is the role of antioxidants in the athlete's diet, especially the relationship between these compounds and muscle damage and soreness. The key antioxidant nutrients are vitamin A (beta-carotene), vitamin C, vitamin E, copper, and selenium. At this time, data are controversial—some studies suggest an increased need for antioxidant nutrients with training, while others do not. Similarly, some report less muscle soreness with supplementation

iStockphoto/Thinkstock

In some states, performing a nutrition assessment and then following it by recommending specific quantities of foods or supplements may be in violation of the law.

of antioxidants, while others do not. All individuals, regardless of whether they are athletes, should eat antioxidant-rich foods for overall health promotion. Some common antioxidant-rich foods are listed in Figure 8-1.

Currently, the data do not support regular supplementation with antioxidant nutrients. Most of the long-term studies examining antioxidants and health focus on cardiovascular disease (CVD). These long-term studies report that antioxidant supplementation is not especially protective against CVD; other lifestyle factors must be studied and considered. However, consuming foods rich in antioxidants (e.g. fruits, vegetables, whole grains) is likely beneficial for better health in all individuals.

When someone is interested in supplements, it is appropriate to share the research data and then let the individual make the decision whether or not to supplement. It is recommended, however, to also educate those with an interest in supplementation about the current UL for each of the antioxidants and recommend that foods rich in antioxidants are consumed instead. The UL can be difficult to reach exclusively with food intake, but relatively easy to meet with supplementation.

Nutrient	Source
Vitamin A (beta-carotene)	Carrot Cantaloupe Papaya Mango Egg yolk
Vitamin C	Citrus fruits Peppers Strawberries Kiwi
Vitamin E	Nuts Seeds Avocados Canola oil Olive oil
Copper	Salmon Sunflower seeds
Selenium	Brazil nuts Tofu Tuna Mushrooms

Figure 8-1. Common antioxidant-rich foods

❑ Calcium and Vitamin D

Other nutrients of concern—especially in young, female athletes—are calcium and vitamin D, which are necessary for bone health. If an athlete has sun exposure and drinks milk, the vitamin D intake may be adequate. However, young adult women need 1,000 mg per day of calcium, and this need may not be met adequately in the diet alone. While it is possible to have enough calcium in the diet, usually 3-5 servings of dairy or calcium-fortified products daily are needed to fulfill the 1,000 mg requirement. Some young women may avoid dairy foods because of the misconception that these are "fattening" foods. Nonfat milk and dairy products are good sources of quality protein and calcium despite the removal of the fat.

Should a calcium and vitamin D supplement be routinely recommended? Caution is needed when recommending supplements. It is appropriate to explain the role of vitamin D and calcium in bone health and their relationships with other diseases or conditions, but the individual who will be taking the supplements needs to make the decision to use them. Individuals considering supplements need to be aware of the UL for vitamin D and calcium and also should consume foods rich in these nutrients.

It cannot be emphasized enough that in many states, assessing the diet and recommending specific amounts of foods or supplements may violate local or state statutes. Recommending foods rich in certain nutrients for overall health promotion is an appropriate approach, however, because this is considered general, nonmedical nutrition information.

Recommending foods rich in certain nutrients for overall health promotion is an appropriate approach because this is considered general, nonmedical nutrition information.

Vitamins and Minerals That May Be Toxic in High Doses

Many of the micronutrients are toxic in high doses and a UL is set based on current research data. It is important that these UL tables are reviewed with the individuals concerned with their current intake. Copies of these tables should be kept on hand to share with those interested in vitamin and mineral supplementation. Being familiar with the layout and terminology of the tables is critical to allow for knowledgeable discussion on the topics. Reaching the UL from food intake alone is rather difficult. If concerns are present regarding toxic doses of the micronutrients, the discussion should focus on oversupplementation instead of dietary consumption.

Phytochemicals and Health

Phytochemicals, while not classified as nutrients, are biologically active compounds that may reduce the risk of certain diseases like heart disease and cancer. Phytochemicals are abundant in whole grains, fruits, and vegetables. While databases are available to find the vitamin or mineral content of a food, the exact quantities of phytochemicals in foods are not readily available. Likewise, at this time, no DRIs or other specific recommendations for daily intakes of phytochemicals exist. The best advice for individuals concerned about meeting "daily phytochemical needs" is to consume a diet rich in whole grains that includes 8-10 servings per day of fruits and vegetables. Another common recommendation is to eat from the rainbow—to eat as many different colors of fruits and vegetables as possible. The vibrant colors of these plants are, in part, due to the phytochemicals found in them.

Some people may find this recommendation difficult to achieve. Knowledge of food portions will be helpful for clarifying serving size: a serving of fruit is approximately one-half cup of juice or a piece of fruit the size of a tennis ball and a serving of vegetables is just one-half cup of cooked or one cup of uncooked leafy greens. It can be challenging for people who currently eat no fruits and vegetables to increase their consumption level to 8-10 servings a day. It is best to set smaller, achievable goals. For example, a fruit smoothie or vegetables as a pizza topping contribute to meeting the goal. Another misconception: only fresh fruits and vegetables contain adequate nutrients. Generally, fruits and vegetables reach their peak nutrient content at their peak ripeness. It can be inconvenient to have to go to the market regularly to purchase produce, and fresh produce seems to spoil very quickly, especially when bought at the perfectly ripe state. Frozen fruits and vegetables are picked and frozen at peak ripeness and immediately packaged. Keeping frozen fruits and vegetables on hand can make it very convenient to incorporate these into the diet by adding frozen berries to a fruit smoothie, yogurt, or slice of angel food cake, or including frozen vegetables in a stir fry, as a pizza topping, or as a side dish.

Some individuals may inquire about taking a supplement containing phytochemicals instead of eating fruits and vegetables. Research in this area is new, without adequate data to establish firm recommendations, but supplementation is still an important point of discussion. The bottom line is that it is not known if taking a phytochemical isolated in pill form will have the same effect as consuming the whole foods that naturally contain them. It could be that the phytochemical in question interacts with other unidentified phytochemicals or antioxidants present in the whole food and when extracted would not have the same beneficial affect. Considering the unknowns, it is better to recommend to concerned individuals that phytochemical needs are best met by the consumption of whole foods rather than phytochemical supplements.

Martin Poole

For overall good health, it is prudent to recommend using whole foods to meet the optimal intakes of micronutrients (including antioxidants) and phytochemicals.

Summary

Dietary Reference Intakes (DRIs) are designed to meet the needs of approximately 97-98% of the healthy population. These values are appropriate for individual use by those who are free of disease or other medical conditions. Athletes and highly active individuals may have slightly higher needs for a few micronutrients. However, these higher micronutrient needs can be met with the increased energy, or calories, required for training. Some nutrients warrant further consideration in athletes and active persons, and while supplementation of these micronutrients may be beneficial, care should be taken. State statutes may prohibit the fitness professional from conducting a nutrition assessment and recommending specific quantities of foods or supplements. For overall good health, it is prudent to recommend using whole foods to meet the optimal intakes of micronutrients (including antioxidants) and phytochemicals.

9

Fluid and Electrolyte Needs

Importance of Water

Approximately 60% of the body is made of water. Water is essential to survival and has the following functions:

- Transportation, as a component of blood and urine
- Removal of waste products
- Protection, serving as a lubricant, cleanser, and cushion
- Involvement in many metabolic reactions
- Temperature regulation (heat loss via sweat)

When a decrease in body water occurs, compensatory responses designed to conserve water take affect. One is decreased saliva production that causes dry mouth and increased thirst. Another is decreased blood volume that leads to decreased blood pressure that signals the brain to increase the thirst mechanism. The kidney also plays an important role by increasing water reabsorption in response to antidiuretic hormone.

Average body water loss is approximately 2.75 L per day. The apparent water losses occur in the form of sweat and urine at about 1-2 L per day, but an additional liter or so can be lost via evaporation in expired breath and from skin. The value is representative of an inactive person at room temperature. For an active person working in a warm environment, water losses can be much greater. The DRI for fluid intake in adults is 2.7 L per day for women and 3.7 L per day for men. These needs vary, depending on the level of physical activity and environmental conditions.

Physical Activity, Health, and Performance

Physical activity can induce increased sweat rates and, therefore, significantly higher water and electrolyte losses, with the magnitude of the losses being greater in a warm environment. Sweat rates vary greatly among individuals and with different types of physical activity. In general, women have lower sweat rates than men, but there may not be significant differences in electrolyte losses between the genders. Children may have lower sweat rates than adults, but the electrolyte losses may also be slightly lower or the same.

If water and electrolytes are not adequately replaced, dehydration will occur, which will result in impaired performance. Decreased body fluid levels at just over 2% of total body weight can lead to increased physiologic strain and perceived effort of the activity, especially in a warm environment. Though the data are not as abundant, dehydration that results in a 3-5% loss of body weight is unlikely to impair anaerobic or strength performance.

In addition to detriments in performance, dehydration can contribute to heat exhaustion and exertional heat stroke, and may increase the chance of developing, or the severity of, acute renal failure. Research data are less clear in supporting the relationship between dehydration and electrolyte loss and muscle cramps, but since fluids and electrolytes are necessary to maintain other physiological functions, it is prudent to ensure adequate intake of these two items.

Stockbyte

Dehydration can contribute to heat exhaustion and exertional heat stroke, and may increase the chance of developing, or the severity of, acute renal failure.

It is important to prevent, as much as possible,
body-weight loss due to water loss during physical activity.

iStockphoto/Thinkstock

Fluid/Electrolyte Needs Before, During, and After Exercise

Beginning an exercise session or athletic event in a euhydrated (adequately hydrated) state is recommended for optimal performance. One of the simplest ways to determine the hydration level is by examining urine color. Urine that is clear or pale yellow is indicative of adequate hydration. If the urine darkens, dehydration is underway. Various urine color charts are available on the Internet and easily can be found using a search engine. To optimize water absorption and allow urine output to stabilize, it is best to begin consuming fluids several hours before physical activity. Beverages with electrolytes are valuable to stimulate thirst and help retain fluids in the body.

It is important to prevent, as much as possible, body-weight loss due to water loss during physical activity. To establish an accurate baseline body weight, a person must be in energy balance (weight stable) and be well-hydrated. Body weight should be measured first thing in the morning, after urinating, and in the nude, for a minimum of three consecutive days. If daily weight is different by more than 1%, additional values should be taken, which is especially important for women, as they will experience body-water fluctuations with the menstrual cycle.

The hydration goal during physical activity is to maintain body weight within 2% of the baseline body weight. For example, a 125-lb female should drink enough to keep her body weight between 122.5 and 125 lb after exercise. Because of variations in sweat rates and other factors—such as the duration of the activity, clothing and equipment, weather, and acclimatization to the environment—no one recommendation exists for all individuals and situations. A suggested starting point is 0.4-0.8 L of fluid per hour. In addition to consuming fluids and electrolytes during physical activity, the presence of carbohydrate in the beverage can help sustain endurance performance by sparing glycogen from being broken down in the body. The lower value for fluid intake (0.4 L) may be more appropriate for slower, smaller individuals, while the upper end (0.8 L) may be best for faster, larger people. Environment will also play a large factor. It is important to use pre- and post-exercise body weights during practice and training sessions to establish an individualized fluid-replacement program. It is vital to pre-plan and practice beforehand since there likely will not be scales available at all times.

Replacing fluid losses after exercise is a priority, but the first thing to consider is subsequent scheduled exercise sessions and athletic events. If an individual finishes a marathon and will not be engaging in further physical activity the rest of the day, adequate rehydration can be achieved by consuming beverages at meal times. On the other hand, situations may arise where more rapid rehydration is necessary. For example, when competing in a tournament it is advisable to consume approximately 1.5 L of fluid for each kilogram lost and to continue to eat appropriate meals or snacks (preferably containing some sodium) throughout the day.

The hydration goal during physical activity is to maintain body weight within 2% of the baseline body weight.

iStockphoto/Thinkstock

The Dangers of Hyponatremia

Hyponatremia is a general medical condition that involves having low serum sodium. Exercise-associated hyponatremia is specific to athletes and usually occurs with long-duration endurance events. Hyponatremia can be a severe medical condition that results in hospitalization or death. Hyponatremia generally occurs by overdrinking of hypotonic fluids (e.g., plain water) that is coupled with excessive sodium losses via sweat. The condition is more common in athletes with large sweat sodium losses who also have low body weights. It is beneficial to consume a sports drink before and during exercise (see Chapter 5 for details) because of the fluid, electrolytes, and carbohydrates supplied.

Beverage Choices

❑ Water

Plain water can meet hydration needs when large amounts of sweat are not lost, as is the case with sedentary or light activities of short duration. The potential problem with plain water is taste—some people may not drink as much as is needed due to the lack of flavor. However, plain water is not appropriate for individuals who lose large amounts of sweat during activity due to the risk of developing hyponatremia. They need the additional electrolytes contained in sports drinks.

❑ Traditional Sports Drinks

Most sports drinks are a 6-8% carbohydrate solution and generally contain approximately 14-15 g of carbohydrate per cup. They also contain the electrolytes sodium, potassium, and chloride and should contain at least 70 mg of sodium per cup. These beverages come in a variety of flavors, are inexpensive, readily accessible, and come in both powdered and liquid forms. Sports drinks are ideal for individuals exercising for longer periods of time (i.e., greater than 45 minutes) and are especially helpful in a warm environment.

❑ Fitness Waters

Fitness waters are lightly flavored, but contain less carbohydrate (generally 3 g per cup) and sodium than a traditional sports drink. People who sweat enough to need fluid replacement, but do not exercise intensely enough to warrant the carbohydrate content of the traditional sports drink, may benefit from using fitness waters. The added flavor in these products may encourage more fluid intake than plain water. Some current products have been fortified with calcium or have added caffeine. The caffeine content is modest and equivalent to diet colas (approximately 20 mg of caffeine per cup). Many of these products are available in both liquid and powder form.

❑ Specialized Sports Drinks

Some sports drinks may have a higher carbohydrate or sodium content than others. For example, individuals who have excessive sodium losses in their sweat may need a specialized product to optimally replenish these losses. Other specialty products contain only half of the carbohydrate content, and retain the same electrolyte concentration of traditional sports drinks. These products are ideal for times of intermittent high- and low-intensity exertion, as with sports that require engagement on the field and then some time off the field.

Summary

Water has many functions, but a key one for athletes and physically active individuals is temperature regulation. Body weight losses of as little as 2% can impair endurance performance. It is important to prevent exercise-induced body-weight loss by consuming fluids before and after exercise. Sweat rates vary from person to person, and each individual must take responsibility for establishing a hydration schedule. Consuming fluids that contain electrolytes is important for the prevention of hyponatremia, and consuming fluids that contain carbohydrates is needed for the prevention of glycogen depletion and, therefore, enhanced endurance performance. Many beverages with added flavor are available that encourage fluid intake and replace the carbohydrate and electrolytes lost with physical exertion.

ENERGY BALANCE AND WEIGHT MANAGEMENT

Part II

Hemera/Thinkstock

10

Energy Balance

For a person to maintain body weight, there must be energy balance, or a situation where energy consumed equals energy expended. If more energy is consumed than is used, weight will be gained; if more energy is expended than consumed, weight will be lost. However, numerous other factors contribute to and affect energy intake and expenditure. Several factors affect energy intake, such as ethnic and religious practices, family traditions, childhood experiences (e.g., foods received as rewards), emotional comfort received from food, access, convenience, availability, variety, education, occupation, income, nutrition beliefs, media or peer influences, and the taste of food. Some factors may not be easily controllable—such as physical disability, injury or other form of activity restriction, and physical environment (e.g., living in an unsafe neighborhood)—while other factors, such as making time for exercise, may be. Although it is relatively easy to describe the concept of energy balance, it is much more difficult to implement it in practice with clients.

Components of Energy Expenditure

Total daily energy expenditure (TDEE) can be broken down into the following three components:

- Resting metabolic rate (RMR), also known as resting energy expenditure (REE)
- Thermic effect of food (TEF), also known as dietary induced thermogenesis (DIT)
- Energy expenditure due to physical activity (EEPA)

If more energy is consumed than is used, weight will be gained; if more energy is expended than consumed, weight will be lost.

❑ Resting Metabolic Rate

RMR, the largest component of the TDEE, represents 60-75% of daily expenditure and is the amount of energy the body expends on maintenance activities while at rest, such as growth and maintenance of tissues, organ function, breathing, circulation, and other bodily activities that keep people alive. Many years of scientific research indicate that a key factor correlated with RMR is lean body mass (LBM), which is made up of muscle, bone, and water. The common saying that "muscle burns more calories than fat" is actually true. Maintaining skeletal muscle requires approximately 13 kcal/kg per day, while adipose tissue requires only 4.5 kcal/kg per day. One effective way to increase RMR is to build skeletal muscle through resistance training. While organs also significantly contribute to RMR, their size or activity cannot be healthily influenced through training or lifestyle modifications, and therefore will not be discussed further.

❑ Thermic Effect of Food

TEF is the energy expended to digest and metabolize food. TEF is the smallest component of TDEE, representing only 5-10% of the total. Because many factors affect this component, TEF needs to be examined carefully. For example, the TEF is a little higher when digesting and metabolizing proteins and carbohydrates as compared to fats. However, this does not mean that unlimited quantities of protein or carbohydrate can be consumed without weight gain. Similarly, TEF is higher for a larger meal as compared with a small snack, but energy expenditure is not significant enough to warrant the frequent consumption of large meals.

Some fad diet books claim that the timing and/or combinations of nutrient consumption will maximize TEF. While the scientific data may support this to an extent, the clinical significance of this theory makes it not entirely worthwhile to attempt to control. Eating these combinations may lead to an increased TEF of only 25 calories per day. It is likely easier to take an extra flight or two of stairs or consume one less piece of hard candy to account for those 25 calories. In addition, measuring TEF is impractical and it is difficult to detect if it is working. Emphasis needs to be placed on the larger picture: decreasing total energy intake and increasing energy expenditure via physical activity.

❏ Energy Expenditure Due to Physical Activity

EEPA represents all voluntary physical activity, including structured exercise, informal activities (e.g., gardening, running errands, housework), and even fidgeting. EEPA is the most variable of the three components of energy expenditure, typically representing 15-30% of the TDEE in most individuals. EEPA can also fall outside of this range. For example, EEPA in a very sedentary person may fall below 15%, while in an elite endurance athlete in training it may be greater than 30%. Of the three components of TDEE, EEPA is the one that is most controllable (unless there is a limiting physical disability present). EPPA is the component where the fitness professional can be most influential with helping clients achieve weight-management goals.

EPPA is the component where the fitness professional can be most influential with helping clients achieve weight-management goals.

Measuring Energy Intake and Expenditure

The overarching goal of a fitness professional in terms of weight management is helping the client balance energy intake with energy expenditure. On the energy intake side of the balance equation, the fitness professional's role is to help clients understand the energy content of the foods consumed and how to best determine this information. On the energy expenditure side, it is the fitness professional's role to determine the mode, frequency, intensity, and duration of physical activity to best meet a client's weight-management goals. As an expert, the fitness professional is qualified and expected to assess fitness levels and program appropriate exercise in accordance with the level of training and certification, giving them great freedom when developing physical-activity programs for clients. In contrast, if a fitness professional is not a registered dietitian, he or she needs to be more cautious when addressing the energy intake side of the equation. The fitness professional's role should be that of an educator rather than a practitioner of dietetics.

The energy content of food is measured by a laboratory technique called bomb calorimetry. A sample of dried food is burned and the amount of heat given off is measured in units called kilocalories (kcal). The kilocalories are in the form of gross energy, which does not take digestibility into consideration. However, the energy values that appear on a food label or in a nutrient database do take digestibility factors into account and the information can be comfortably used by consumers. For example, foods high in fiber are not fully digested in a human body, but are completely combusted in a bomb calorimeter. Therefore, the amount of kilocalories shown on a food label or listed in the USDA nutrient database are invariably less than those measured in a bomb calorimeter. Fortunately, clients will not need to know this detail and can confidently use food labels when making meal choices.

Similar to how heat emission from food burned in a bomb calorimeter is used to determine its energy content, heat production during physical activity is used to estimate energy expenditure in a room calorimeter. This direct measure of energy expenditure is accurate; however, due to its high cost and relative scarcity, it is rarely used in practice. An alternative method to direct calorimetry involves the collection of inspired and expired air and subsequent analysis of oxygen consumption and carbon dioxide production during rest or physical activity. This method is used widely in both research and clinical practice. A third method, called doubly-labeled water, is very accurate for measuring energy expenditure in a free-living environment for several days. Unlike the relative confinement of a room calorimeter, this method allows the estimation of energy expended as people live their normal lives, such as performing activities of daily living and formal physical activity. It is, however, very expensive and few laboratories have the resources at this time to practice this method. Data from this sophisticated methodology were used to establish some of the energy expenditure estimates discussed in Chapter 2.

The fitness professional who wants to help clients achieve their weight-management goals must be able to program a suitable level of exercise to balance their energy-intake level. While performing a complete nutrition assessment is not usually within the scope of practice for a fitness professional, a client's energy needs can be safely estimated using the various equations discussed in Chapter 2 and in the appendices. It is important to emphasize that all of the equations give estimates, not exact energy requirements. The estimates are a good starting point to determine how much to eat in order to meet goals (i.e., weight loss or maintenance) or how many calories are burned during an exercise session. If weight gain or weight loss is occurring, then the person is not in energy balance, even if the equations indicate otherwise. The next step would be to adjust the exercise program or energy needs estimate accordingly. In addition to the fitness professional's guidance, clients can use the MyPyramid website to track energy balance for up to one year. It is a free service provided by the USDA and will require going through a simple process to set up a user account.

iStockphoto/Thinkstock

The fitness preofessional should focus on the energy expenditure side of the energy balance equation by programming appropriate exercise regimens.

Summary

If weight is stable, an individual is in energy balance. The three components of total daily energy expenditure are resting metabolic rate, thermic effect of food, and energy expenditure due to physical activity. Resting metabolic rate is the largest component of total expenditure, but physical activity is the most variable. Both energy content of food and energy expenditure can be estimated using various techniques. Fitness professionals should help healthy clients learn about the energy content of foods by teaching them how to use a food label and using other resources, such as MyPyramid. More importantly, the fitness professional should focus on the energy-expenditure side of the energy-balance equation by programming appropriate exercise regimens.

11

Body Composition

Most definitions of body composition attempt to compartmentalize the body into fat versus fat-free mass (FFM) or lean body mass (LBM). The terms FFM and LBM are often used interchangeably, but technically LBM equals the FFM plus essential fat. Some individuals may equate LBM with only skeletal muscle mass. However, it is important to note that there are three components of LBM: muscle (skeletal muscle and organs), bone, and water. This information will become clearer as methodologies are explained in detail.

Measurement of Body Composition

Many people are interested in what their percent body fat is, and many methods can be used to estimate this value. It is important to know about the currently available techniques as well as the limitations associated with each of these methods. To understand the individual methods, the concept of body compartments must be introduced. A two-compartment body-composition model is one that works from the assumption that the human body is composed of two distinct substances: fat and lean tissue. For example, if a person is found to possess 25% body fat, then he is presumed to also possess 75% LBM, which is the remaining nonfat body mass. A downfall of this model is that the components of LBM (skeletal muscle, bone, and water) are not distinguished, and in this case LBM may be equated with only skeletal muscle mass. Of the three LBM components, water is likely to fluctuate rapidly as hydration status changes. If a research study concludes that an intervention (e.g., exercise program or dietary supplement) resulted in an increased LBM that was measured using a two-compartment method, the increase may have been due to water increases, not skeletal muscle increases. Examples of these two-compartment methods include skinfold analysis and underwater weighing.

A three-compartment model uses the traditional two-compartment model but adds an independent assessment of a third compartment. For example, researchers often use underwater weighing to determine fat and LBM, then use another method, such as isotope dilution, to isolate water from LBM. Using the same example from the previous paragraph, when intervention results in an increased LBM, the amount of body water is known and it can now be concluded that the components of LBM that changed were muscle or bone. If the intervention was a short-term study (e.g., 8 weeks), chances are that bone did not change, as it takes some time for that to happen. It is also likely that body organs did not grow. In this case, it would be safe to assume the LBM increase was in fact due to skeletal muscle. The most accurate method, a four-compartment model, measures fat, skeletal muscle, bone, and water independently. Though the four-compartment model is the most accurate, research studies do not routinely use this model, as some of the methodology is complicated, has limited availability, and is very expensive.

❏   Ideal Body Weight and Body Mass Index

Ideal body weight (IBW), or desirable body weight, indicates the body weight associated with the lowest risk of death. Many height-weight charts or equations exist that purportedly estimate IBW. The primary problem with these standards is that they do not discriminate between overweight and overfat. For example, a lean body builder may weigh far more than "ideal," but may have an extremely low body-fat level. On the other hand, a person may be in the "ideal" weight range, but still have a high body-fat percentage.

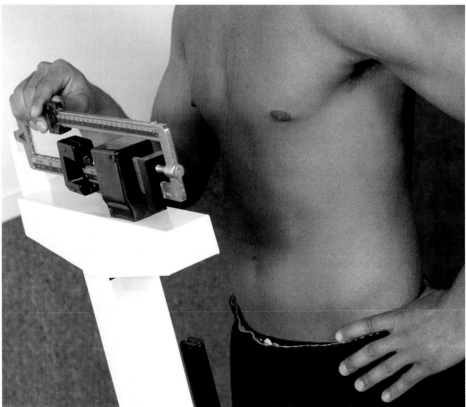

Ideal body weight (IBW), or desirable body weight, indicates the body weight associated with the lowest risk of death.

Body mass index (BMI) is an expression of weight to height ratio (body weight in kilograms divided by height in meters squared). It has a positive correlation with percent body fat, but like the height-weight charts it does not distinguish between overweight and overfat. A BMI of 20-25 is associated with the lowest risk of death, while BMIs above 25 indicate an increased risk of chronic disease. Use BMI with caution, especially in an athletic population. A lean, large person is likely to have a BMI greater than 25, but will have a healthy body composition.

❑ Underwater Weighing

Underwater weighing (UWW) is a technique that has been around for many years and is still considered the "gold standard" by some. The term gold standard refers to the idea that this method was established first, and that the results from UWW were used to gauge the effectiveness of subsequent methods. For example, most equations used to predict body composition from skinfold thickness measurements were validated by actual body-composition measures obtained by using the UWW technique. At best, these secondary methods can be only as accurate as the "gold standard" upon which they were based.

UWW involves using water displacement to measure body volume. Body mass (weight) and body volume can be used to calculate body density; body density then can be used to estimate percent body fat. Simply put, fat mass is less dense than water, while LBM is denser than water; thus, fat floats and lean tissue sinks. Similarly, a lean person will weigh more underwater than a person with more body fat. The UWW technique requires extensive equipment that is not easily transported. A good system can cost as much as $50,000, and is generally limited to a research setting. Some portable UWW systems exist, but technicians using such systems must take care to calibrate the equipment after transport.

In order to maximize the accuracy of the UWW technique, there must be a measure of residual lung volume (the air left in the lungs after maximal voluntary exhalation). Humans are incapable of fully exhaling all the air in the lungs; in fact, the lungs would collapse if humans were actually successful in this endeavor. Residual air makes the body lighter underwater since air trapped in the lungs increases a body's buoyancy. Failure to correct for this phenomenon results in overestimation of body fatness. An accurate UWW test assumes that the person undergoing the test will exhale completely while underwater. In practice, this is rarely accomplished because the natural instinct is to hold the breath underwater, not exhale what little air is left in the lungs. It is important to keep this in mind when interpreting the results of an UWW test. Also, consider whether residual lung volume is measured directly or estimated using mathematical equations, the latter of which is not as accurate as the former.

UWW systems that use a cadaver scale may be available at the side of a swimming pool. The accuracy of this is also in question because the waves from the pool may cause the needle of the scale to move quickly, preventing the test technician from taking an accurate reading.

It is important to emphasize that no body-composition measurement is 100% accurate.

If sound equipment is used by a trained technician, body composition can be estimated using UWW within approximately 2.5% of actual composition. If a person is measured at 20% fat, he may actually be between 17.5 and 22.5% fat. An advantage of this method is that people of all sizes can be measured (as long as the tank is large enough). In the research setting, it is common to test a lean person who is seven feet tall or an obese individual who weighs 400 pounds. The disadvantages of the method include the sophisticated, expensive equipment and that test subjects must be completely submerged underwater, which may not be comfortable for some individuals.

It is important to emphasize that no body-composition measurement is 100% accurate—this is not possible in a living human being. All of the available methodologies are only estimates of actual body composition.

❑ Skinfolds

The skinfold technique requires the use of a skinfold caliper. The goal is to separate the subcutaneous fat from the muscle and measure the thickness of that fold. The skinfold values are then placed into an equation that will predict body fat. Hundreds of prediction equations are available, and it is important to be familiar with them, or at least with some of the key points. Generalized equations are those developed on large populations and can be used for people of different genders and ages. Population-specific equations are developed on specific groups of people and cannot be transferred to individuals outside that group. For example, an equation developed on a young, lean, female athlete cannot be used with any accuracy on a male football player. When choosing an equation to use, it is important to know how the equation was developed, which may require consulting the scientific literature and making sure the population used is appropriate.

In order to maximize the accuracy of the skinfold technique, there are a few things to consider. First, it is critical to use a high-quality skinfold caliper, which can cost approximately $200. Second, appropriate skinfold sites must be selected and measured. Many references demonstrate the exact anatomical location of the common skinfold sites. For example, to measure the tricep skinfold, any area on the back of the arm will not suffice, as the correct anatomical site must be used. Third, the person taking the measurement must be trained. Measuring skinfolds is not hard to do, but it takes practice. Some skinfolds are easy to take while others are not. People may have sites with fat that is very hard to separate from the muscle. If a good fold cannot be grasped, perhaps an equation that does not use that site should be used. If this is not possible, then the estimation of body fat will be adversely affected. Fourth, the skinfold technique may not be appropriate for obese individuals. The caliper is only so large, and it is often difficult to identify bony landmarks to get the precise fold. Finally, it is essential to choose and use an appropriate equation. It is possible to have a male client with very lean, muscular arms but a large amount of fat in the abdomen. If an equation measuring just arms and not the abdomen was used, body fat may be underpredicted. For a woman who has a very lean upper body but very heavy thighs, using an equation that required only upper-body skinfolds may underestimate her total body fat. Even if the measurement is perfect (equipment, sites, ease, appropriate equation), the error still can be approximately 3.5%.

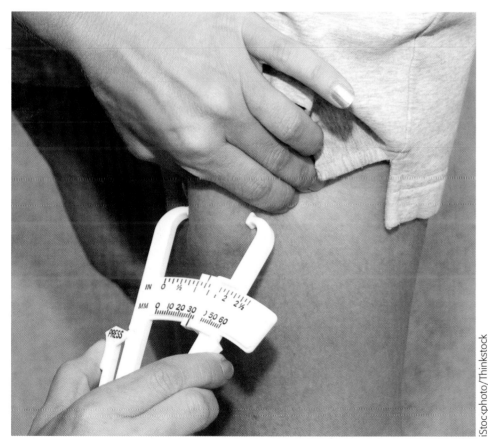

iStockphoto/Thinkstock

Measuring skinfolds is not hard to do, but it takes practice.

❏ Bioelectrical Impedance Analysis

Bioelectrical impedance analysis (BIA) requires a specialized analyzer that can range greatly in terms of quality and cost. A lower-end analyzer can cost $40, while a research-grade instrument can cost up to $5,000. Some analyzers require standing on a scale-like device barefoot or holding handles with bare hands, while the research-quality machines generally require lying down with electrodes placed on the hands and ankles.

The principle of this technique is that an electrical current is passed through the body, and resistance to that current is measured. The greater the percent body fat, the higher the resistance to the electrical current. Fat resists electricity, as it is an insulator, while LBM conducts electricity because it contains water and electrolytes.

This equipment is portable and easy to use, but there are some limitations. Similar to skinfolds, there are prediction equations in the literature that translate the resistance value to a percent body fat. Selecting and using an appropriate equation is required. However, the less-expensive machines will not provide this information. The equipment is also very sensitive to body-water changes and the test must be done in a euhydrated state. The minimum error using this technique is approximately 3.5%, but can vary with the equipment used.

❏ Plethysmography

Plethysmography, a newer technique, uses air displacement to estimate body fat. As with the UWW technique, plethysmography utilizes the principle that body mass (weight) and body volume can be used to calculate body density. Body density can then be used to estimate percent body fat. The makers of the BOD POD™ were the first to successfully market a product that uses plethysmography. The BOD POD™ is an expensive device, costing approximately $60,000. While the technique is a more recent development, the available scientific data suggest that plethysmography is an accurate technique (error of approximately 2.2-3.7%, but more research is needed). Because of the cost, the technique is usually limited to a research setting.

❏ Dual-Energy X-ray Absorptiometry

Dual-energy x-ray absorptiometry (DEXA or DXA) was first developed for the measurement of bone density. DXA is commonly used to assess whole-body bone density as well as that of the hip and spine, which are common sites for osteoporotic fractures. DXA can be used to diagnose a person with osteopenia or osteoporosis. A secondary benefit to this technique is that is gives a fairly accurate percent body fat estimate (<2% error, depending on the model of the machine), though more research is needed to confirm the accuracy.

While the accuracy is quite acceptable, there are several limitations to this technique. First, the cost is greater than $100,000 with additional extensive maintenance costs. Second, there is radiation exposure to the person being measured. While the radiation dose is very small, it requires strict regulation and therefore the machine can be housed only in a medical or university setting. State regulations vary in that some states require a licensed operator while others do not. Either way, the operator must regularly undergo DXA and radiation safety training. To receive the test, a physician's prescription is usually required. Finally, the DXA scanner can hold a maximum of 300 lb and the table size is limited. If a person cannot be placed properly on the table due to large body dimensions, the test cannot be done with accuracy.

❑ Total Body Water

Total body water (TBW) is most accurately measured in a laboratory or medical setting. It requires the use of radioisotopes and collection of either urine or blood. Though a fairly accurate measure of TBW can be obtained, the equipment to analyze the samples is quite expensive. TBW can be estimated using BIA, but generally the results are not as accurate as the radioisotope techniques.

Interpreting Body Composition Results

It is important to understand that no body-composition assessment technique is 100% accurate and to select the best method based on availability, cost, and accuracy. When discussing the results of body composition measurement, it is important to include the error range (e.g., a measurement of 20% fat may actually be 17% or 23%, depending on the method). Noting the error range is especially important when pre- and post-intervention measures are taken.

Is it really important for individuals to know their body-fat percentage? For some competitive athletes, the answer is yes. Perhaps it is a motivating factor for these individuals. The value is also very important in research projects measuring the effects of a particular intervention. How important is it for the general population to know this information? As mentioned above, it may be a motivating factor. If body-composition measures are used regularly, enough time should be available between measures to detect results, considering the potential error. While this is logical to the fitness professional, it may not be so to those with whom they work. For example, if individuals work very hard to lose body fat and eight weeks later they have gained 0.5% body fat, their motivation could be destroyed. Though the 0.5% gain is within the error of the methodology, the person working to lose body fat may not see it that way. Unless body-composition changes can be visually detected, it may be best to focus on other areas, like improved fitness levels or the fit and feel of clothing.

To measure body composition as a baseline, it is important to know acceptable body-fat standards. One set of standards is presented in the sixth edition of the *American College of Sports Medicine's Resource Manual for Guidelines for Exercise Testing and Prescription* and is summarized in Figure 11-1.

It is important to be familiar with these standards, since the general population may not be. For example, it is not uncommon to measure a young athletic woman at 20% fat, and have her feel that the value is rather high. Some women may believe that they need to have percent body fat values in the single digits. However, body-fat measures that are that low are detrimental to health. The young woman in the example would need to be educated that her body fat is indeed normal and healthy. Many people, especially athletes, are under the belief that the lower the percent body fat, the better they will perform. While it is true that being lean is a benefit in some sports (e.g., distance running), having too little body fat can be detrimental to performance. It is critical to encourage all individuals to maintain body-fat levels in the appropriate range.

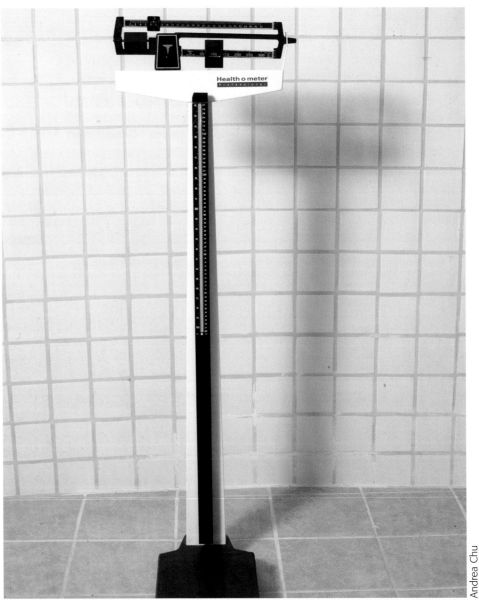

If body-composition measures are used regularly, enough time should be available between measures to detect results, considering the potential error.

Men	% Fat*
Essential	3-5
Minimal	5
Athletic	5-13
Recommended (≤34 years)	8-22
Recommended (35-55 years)	10-25
Recommended (+56 years)	10-25
Women	**% Fat***
Essential	8-12
Minimal	10-12
Athletic	12-22
Recommended (≤34 years)	20-35
Recommended (35-55 years)	23-38
Recommended (+56 years)	25-38

Figure 11-1. Body-fat standards as presented in *ACSM's Resource Manual for Guidelines for Exercise Testing and Prescription*, sixth edition. *Percent values greater than recommended indicate overweight or obesity.

❏ Healthy Body Weight

In addition to body-fat values that must be measured, some people are likely to ask about healthy body weight. Tables and equations are available to help determine desirable body weight, but limitations exist. Individuals concerned about their desirable or ideal body weight may have unrealistic goals (e.g., to return to their high school body weight). It is important for the fitness professional to discuss the concept of healthy body weight, while not focusing on numbers. A functional definition of healthy body weight is the weight where the person feels good, is free of disease or can manage chronic disease, and can perform physical activity comfortably. The healthy body-weight value may differ from a chart or from a previous weight. A person who is overweight with a chronic disease should set a goal to return to the body weight where he was free of symptoms (e.g., normal lipids, glucose, or blood pressure). Some people who have type 2 diabetes can control their blood glucose with weight management, balanced nutrient intake, and regular physical activity.

❏ Calculating a Target Body Weight for a Given Body-Fat Level

In some situations, it may be appropriate to measure body composition regularly and set a goal percent body fat to optimize performance. To perform this calculation, a baseline body-composition measurement is needed. This calculation is based on a constant LBM. The following formula should be used:

Desired Body Weight = Current LBM / (1 − Desired % Body Fat)

Example: 200-lb male with 20% body fat (80% LBM). The goal is 15% body fat.

Determine LBM: 200 lb x 0.80 = 160 lb LBM

Desired Body Weight: 160 lb / (1 − .15) = 160 / 0.85 = 188 lb

Summary

Many techniques exist to measure body composition, with the accuracy and availability varying with each method. It is important to understand the limitations and inherent errors of each method and to help interested individuals properly interpret the results.

12

Weight-Loss Strategies

The health consequences of being overweight or obese are available from many sources. In this area, the Centers for Disease Control and Prevention (CDC) is a leading authority (www.cdc.gov). According to the CDC, 65% of American adults are overweight or obese, with an average weight gain of 1.75 lb (0.8 kg) each year. Overweight or obesity is associated with an increased risk for many chronic diseases, including the following:

- Type 2 diabetes
- Hypertension
- Dyslipidemia and cardiovascular disease
- Gallbladder disease
- Osteoarthritis
- Some cancers
- Sleep apnea

One way of defining overweight and obesity in an individual is the use of the body mass index (BMI). While BMI has limitations when used in some individuals, it is a reasonable tool to use when categorizing overweight and obesity in populations; a BMI of 25-29.9 is considered overweight, while a BMI of 30 or greater is indicative of obesity.

Both environmental and genetic factors contribute to obesity. While research is in the early stages, it appears that several physiological factors also play a role. For example, adipose tissue is not only a stagnant place to store fat. It appears to secrete hormones, such as leptin, which may play a role in satiety. Another hormone secreted by the stomach, ghrelin, may contribute to obesity by increasing appetite. Genetics may play a role as well. The offspring of normal-weight parents have a 10% chance of becoming obese. If one or both parents are obese, this chance is increased to 40% or 80%, respectively.

While genetics and physiology contribute to body-weight regulation, the population-wide weight gain seen in the United States is also likely due to cultural influences that encourage a chronic energy imbalance due to excess food intake and/or decreased physical activity. A strong inverse relationship exists between obesity and levels of physical activity and fitness levels; less active and unfit individuals have a greater risk for becoming obese. Similarly, people who engage in more physical activity and are fit tend to gain less weight over time. Fitness professionals play a critical role in encouraging the general population to maintain appropriate levels of physical activity for health and exercise performance. However, the energy intake side of the equation must also be examined.

Principles of Weight Management

As previously indicated, energy balance is critical for weight management. While being out of balance for a short time will not lead to significant weight changes, chronic energy imbalance will lead to weight loss or gain. Though the statement that 3,500 calories equals one pound of fat is not 100% metabolically accurate, it is appropriate for the fitness professional's practical purposes. To lose a pound of fat in one week, a person must be in an energy deficit of 500 calories per day (3,500 calories/seven days). The deficit can be achieved through reduced energy intake, increased energy expenditure, or, ideally, both. Similarly, a person wanting to gain weight (muscle mass) needs to consume an additional 400-500 calories per day and participate in an appropriate strength-training regimen. While a simple concept in theory, implementing it may not be easy.

Fitness professionals play a critical role in encouraging the general population to maintain appropriate levels of physical activity for health and exercise performance.

iStockphoto/Thinkstock

Sound weight-loss plans are those that control energy intake and promote regular physical activity, while instilling lifelong changes in habits.

Sound weight-loss plans are those that control energy intake and promote regular physical activity, while instilling lifelong changes in habits. Individuals seeking to lose weight may not recognize that the weight gain possibly took years, and may expect weight loss to be quick and easy. This perspective is not surprising considering all of the media claims about how easy weight loss can be with a particular diet or pill. Sometimes it can be challenging to convince clients that lifelong habit changes are crucial for weight loss and maintenance. A sound weight-loss plan generally has the following characteristics:

- Promotes a slow and steady weight loss (e.g., one pound per week)
- A weight loss of approximately 10% of body weight is followed by a three- to six-month period of weight maintenance
- Encourages common foods
- Allows the individual to participate in social events and eat at restaurants
- Allows flexibility for individual food preferences
- Restricts energy while other nutrient needs are met
- Promotes lifelong changes in habits
- Includes social support
- Does not eliminate certain foods or whole food groups
- Is science-based
- Encourages regular physical activity

Caution should be taken with any diet plan that promotes the use of weight-loss supplements, requires the purchase of special foods, or makes unrealistic claims. While it is necessary to answer questions about some popular fad diets, it is more important to evaluate and discuss the scientific evidence behind all of the popular plans and claims to determine if a particular plan is sound.

Fad Diets

When people want to lose weight, one of the first things they turn to is a popular diet, and, with many diet books on the shelves and diet plans on the Internet, it can be overwhelming. In addition, many diet books and plans promise to be the last diet a person will ever need and that the unwanted pounds will melt away. If losing weight was as easy as these diets claim, the obesity epidemic in this county would be a nonissue. It is difficult for any health professional to thoroughly read every diet book on the market. However, understanding some of the principles in popular diet books is warranted before having a discussion about specific diet plans.

❑ Carbohydrate-Restricted Diets

Carbohydrate-restricted diets vary in the amount of the daily carbohydrate "allowed," but the amount often ranges from 20 to 90 g per day. These diets usually allow unlimited protein and fat. The common claims in these diets are that consuming carbohydrates leads to weight gain and that insulin is an undesirable anabolic hormone that promotes fat storage. It is important to examine these statements with clients interested in these types of diets. Is it a true statement that eating carbohydrates will make people fat? It is only partially true. Carbohydrates will lead to weight gain if more are consumed than the body burns for fuel or stores as glycogen, but making a blanket statement that consuming carbohydrates leads to a gain in body fat is inappropriate. Consider elite runners. They are not fat, but they do eat lots of carbohydrate. However, elite runners burn what is consumed. If more carbohydrate is consumed than is being used, the anabolic hormone insulin will promote fat storage. The books and diets that promote carbohydrate restriction fail to mention that insulin also plays a role in skeletal muscle protein synthesis. Partial truths must be pointed out when discussing these types of fad diets to prevent people from being afraid to consume carbohydrates.

Do these diets work? If you look at simply pounds lost, then the answer is a resounding "yes" in the first 7-10 days. The problem is that much of the weight reduction is due to loss of body water, not body fat. With restricted carbohydrate intake, glycogen becomes depleted, and body water is lost. For every gram of glycogen stored in the body, almost 3 g of water is stored with it. The glycogen stores are used in the initial days of the diet, which will result in water loss. The outcomes of a few short-term studies have reported more weight loss with low-carbohydrate diets. However, studies that are longer (6-12 months) show no benefit of a low-carbohydrate diet over other types of diets. According to these studies, the key factors for weight loss were energy restriction and exercise. A few more recent studies have examined the role of protein, independent of carbohydrate intake, on weight loss. Some preliminary data suggest that higher protein intakes (still within the DRI) may be associated with slight increases in energy expenditure, which may result in greater satiation. More data are needed before absolute conclusions can be made.

Are there any adverse health effects to consuming a low-carbohydrate diet? The answer to this question is not quite clear. In the short-term, it is unlikely, but, due to the lack of well-controlled, long-term research studies, less is known about chronic reduced consumption. When carbohydrate intake is restricted to the point that glycogen stores are depleted, the body will try to use fat for fuel. Carbohydrate is needed for the complete breakdown of a fatty acid molecule. When carbohydrate is not available, the fatty acid molecules will partially break down, and then turn to an alternate, available pathway. The result is the formation of ketone bodies. While the brain and nervous tissue function better with carbohydrate as a fuel source, ketones can be used as a backup fuel. Because ketones are acids, excessive production of ketones is considered unhealthy and could lead to ketoacidosis, a dangerous metabolic condition that can result in coma or death. Fortunately, the ketone levels from dietary carbohydrate restriction usually do not reach the dangerous levels that are seen in a person with diabetes. People trying to adhere to the limits in the carbohydrate-restricted diets sometimes may consume additional carbohydrates, keeping the ketone levels reasonable. Ketones also help suppress appetite, which may lead to some people still choosing this method of dieting.

While ketones can be used to an extent as a fuel source, the brain and nervous tissue still need some glucose. As previously noted, glucose cannot be synthesized from fatty acids (only a small amount from the glycerol backbone). However, glucose can be synthesized from glucogenic amino acids. It is unclear how carbohydrate-restricted diets affect body composition. Is the protein consumed in the diet being used to make glucose instead of other items? Is skeletal muscle being catabolized to make glucose for the brain in the absence of carbohydrate? More research studies are needed before these questions can be accurately answered.

Some health consequences may occur from following the diet, specifically related to the development of chronic disease. If the diet is high in healthy fats (poly- and monounsaturated), then hyperlipidemia may not be an issue. If,

It is unclear how carbohydrate-restricted diets affect body composition.

however, a large amount of saturated or trans fats are consumed, then dyslipidemia may be a side effect. While studies have shown these diets do not have a negative affect on blood lipids, limitations exist. The studies were short-term in length, and, therefore, the effects of adhering to this type of diet long-term are unknown. Furthermore, the factor of weight loss itself must be considered. If a person loses weight, no matter what method is used, serum cholesterol generally will be lowered. It is less clear whether or not this drop in serum cholesterol will be maintained, and more importantly, whether it translates to a reduced risk of developing cardiovascular disease. More research studies are needed in this area, and other factors that may influence the serum lipid profile, such as heredity, dietary intake, and physical-activity patterns, need to be examined. Another factor to consider is that these diets can fail to provide adequate amounts of some key nutrients for health, including calcium, magnesium, potassium, antioxidants, and phytochemicals. As discussed in Chapter 6, no concrete answers are available to define the relationship between diet and cancer. However, some data exist that support that populations who consume diets high in animal products and low in plant foods have an increased risk for developing some cancers. The Dietary Approaches to Stop Hypertension (DASH; www.dashdiet.org) trials showed that diets moderate in sodium, and rich in fruits and vegetables, and that include low-fat dairy and lean protein were effective in improving blood pressure. The low-carbohydrate diets lack many of these nutrients. Diets that are more carbohydrate controlled (rather than carbohydrate restricted) generally promote intake of quality carbohydrates, lean protein sources, and healthy fats. However, some plans still have restrictions of certain foods or food groups without any scientific rationale.

Some limitations exist with the currently available studies. First, one macronutrient level cannot be manipulated without affecting another one (if one is increased, another is decreased). In this case, it is difficult to attribute any weight changes to one of the nutrients. Second, leaner individuals lose more lean body mass per unit of body weight than those who have more body fat. Furthermore, men may lose more lean body mass per unit of body weight than women. It is important for research studies to have well-matched subjects if weight loss or body composition is a study outcome.

Until strong research data support a different recommendation for weight loss, it is wise is to encourage carbohydrate, fat, and protein ratios consistent with the following current DRIs for macronutrients (Appendix C2): 45-65% carbohydrate, 10-35% protein, and 20-35% fat. Adequate protein intake (within the DRI range) coupled with resistance training may help maintain lean body mass during periods of weight loss. The wide ranges allow for individual responses to macronutrient patterns and encourages individual meal-planning choices.

❑ Food Combining

Some diet plans emphasize that eating specific foods in the proper combination will result in weight loss. For example, many plans promote not consuming carbohydrates, fats, or proteins at the same time because the digestive enzymes responsible for these nutrients will cancel each other out and the digestive process will be altered. If not digested in the small intestine, carbohydrates, fats, and proteins go to the large intestine and ultimately out of the body. Any macronutrient not absorbed in the small intestine will eventually be excreted in the feces. From a weight-loss standpoint, it would be great to be able to eat carbohydrates, proteins, and fats at the same time and have the calories canceled out. Some of these diets take it further and suggest that beverage consumption, specifically water, with meals dilutes the digestive enzymes and renders them ineffective. If this were true a large meal of pizza and soda could be consumed, and the calories would filter through the body without affecting it. In fact, water is already present in the digestive tract to aid in the digestive process and is then reabsorbed into the body. If it were possible, this diet method would certainly be a very unhealthy mode of weight loss, but in some sense a dream to the dieter. Not withstanding the fact that there are no research data to support this concept, it physiologically does not make sense.

Stockbyte

Some data exist that support that populations who consume diets high in animal products and low in plant foods have an increased risk for developing some cancers.

Many people can lose weight for a time, but what percentage of those who do are able to keep the weight off?

❏ Weight Loss versus Weight Maintenance

Most fad diets will result in weight loss because they are inherently low in calories. In addition, many individuals trying to lose weight can tolerate food restrictions for short periods of time. While it is a proven fact that obesity is associated with the risk of developing many chronic diseases and that weight loss can improve health, some individuals may not consider the importance of weight maintenance. Many people can lose weight for a time, but what percentage of those who do are able to keep the weight off? Given the current obesity epidemic, it seems that few individuals succeed at weight-loss maintenance.

Some of the most compelling data available at this time come from the National Weight Control Registry (NWCR; www.nwcr.ws/). The NWCR, created in 1994, is the largest research investigation of successful weight loss maintenance. The NWCR has data on more than 5,000 individuals who have lost significant amounts of weight and maintained that weight loss for extended periods of time. The overall conclusion thus far is that the successful participants in the study have two common courses of action—dietary and physical-activity modification. Dietary modification includes changes like eating breakfast daily and using portion control, while the physical-activity patterns include exercising approximately one hour per day and watching television less than 10 hours per week. Regular body-weight measurements also seem to be a motivating factor.

While the fact that little data are available to support fad diets, some strong evidence exists to support lifestyle changes, such as portion control and regular physical activity, and it is important to convey this message. A fitness professional plays a critical role in establishing exercise recommendations and guidelines that will keep clients motivated to be physically active most days of the week.

Limitations With Fad Diets

No significant scientific research exists to support a specific fad diet plan. In fad diets, the ease of weight loss is promised, often without exercise, and foods or food groups are forbidden or restricted. The diets may be inadequate for health and balanced nutrition. They are also generally hard to plan for, since changes in habits are required overnight and participants are encouraged to follow the rules rather than develop habits that can be sustained long term.

Any diet book or plan that promotes easy weight loss without exercise should be viewed with caution. Fortunately, many good books and plans are available that teach sensible eating strategies with an emphasis on macronutrient balance and portion control. The DRIs and MyPyramid (see Appendix C2; www.mypyramid.gov) are excellent resources for healthy individuals to use for assessing their personal energy balance and developing a portion-controlled meal plan on their own. Someone with a disease or other medical condition (e.g., diabetes, cardiovascular disease, or hypertension) who is seeking weight-loss advice should be referred to a registered dietitian for individualized meal planning.

Someone with a disease or other medical condition (e.g., diabetes, cardiovascular disease, or hypertension) who is seeking weight-loss advice should be referred to a registered dietitian for individualized meal planning.

Weight Loss and Body Composition

From the available literature on diets, it appears that the macronutrient distribution is not as important as total energy intake when attempting to lose weight. In addition to total weight loss, it is important to consider the composition of the weight lost. A negative energy balance results in weight loss from a reduction in both fat mass and lean body mass, with the losses of lean body mass being significant with more severe energy restriction.

Some individuals wanting to lose weight may have the goal of reducing body fat while simultaneously gaining lean body mass, specifically muscle mass. It would difficult to achieve this goal because dieting puts the body in a

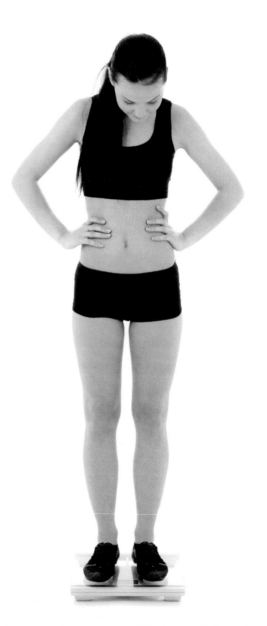

Weight loss is easier to accomplish than weight maintenance.

state of catabolism, but to facilitate muscle mass gain the body needs to be in a state of anabolism. It is prudent to encourage an appropriate weight loss (1-2 pounds per week) through modest energy restriction and physical activity. An example of this would be to create a 500 kcal/day energy deficit by reducing energy intake and increasing energy expenditure.

Some individuals may want to lose weight very quickly and turn to low-calorie meal plans to accomplish this goal. In this case, the proportion of lean body mass loss may be greater than body-fat loss. A higher percent body fat may result even though body weight was lost. This relative increase in fat with the concomitant reduction in lean body mass may be discouraging to those individuals trying to lose weight. In addition to the inherent error, this fluctuation is another reason to be careful with regular measures of body composition.

As mentioned previously, weight loss is easier to accomplish than weight maintenance. The following are general strategies for successful weight loss and weight maintenance:

- *Initial weight loss goals should be approximately 10% of body weight.* This loss should be achieved through a modest energy deficit (e.g., 500 kcal/day) created by calorie control and increased physical activity.
- *Once 10% of the body weight is lost, ideally the person should work to maintain that weight loss for approximately three months.* Once the three months are finished, the person can reevaluate his body weight and set a new goal of 10% weight loss. Individuals seeking to lose weight may want to lose as much weight as possible in the shortest amount of time. By losing weight in stages, they are more likely to develop permanent lifestyle habits that translate into long-term body-weight maintenance.
- *Regular physical activity may not result in a simultaneous decrease in body fat and increase in lean body mass.* However, an appropriate exercise program consisting of aerobic exercise and strength training can increase the likelihood of maintaining lean body mass during the energy deficit period.

❏ Weight Cycling

Weight cycling occurs when people experience repeating periods of weight loss and weight gain. Usually, people who are motivated by the diet fad of the month are initially intrigued by the novelty, experience no long-term habit changes, and ultimately go back to their old habits. When people lose weight, they lose not only fat, but also lean body mass, especially if exercise is not part of the plan. When they gain the weight back, it is primarily in the form of fat, assuming that exercise is still not part of the lifestyle. This chronic loss of lean body mass and gain of body fat results in an altered body composition such that after years of weight cycling, body weight may be the same, but the percent body fat is higher. This alteration in body composition will likely make it even harder to lose or maintain weight because resting metabolism may also be lowered. It is better to lose a few pounds and maintain it for a long period than to chronically lose and gain larger quantities of body mass.

Weight-Loss Supplements

Similar to the promises of diet books, many claims are made by supplement manufacturers regarding easy weight loss—no counting calories, and, often, no required exercise. Individuals already interested in the products may expect confirmation of all of those false promises. It is the responsibility of a fitness professional to provide accurate, current information about the safety and efficacy of the products in question (see Chapter 2 for more details on discussing supplements). At the same time, extensive reading is required to keep current with all of the scientific literature, and it is essential to have appropriate reference materials. If unsure about a particular product, it is perfectly acceptable to refer the interested client to a more knowledgeable professional or to get back to the client once more information is known. A few of the major categories of weight-loss supplements are presented in the following sections. Only a few key points to consider are included in the sections. If more information is needed, more comprehensive reviews should be consulted.

It is the responsibility of a fitness professional to provide accurate, current information about the safety and efficacy of supplement products that are available on the market.

❑ Carnitine

Carnitine is a compound that aids the transport of fatty acids across the mitochondrial membrane for oxidation (breakdown). The theory is that ingesting the compound results in increased fatty acid oxidation, and hence fat loss. The body naturally makes carnitine, and research data do not support its effectiveness in increasing fat loss.

❑ Chromium Picolinate

Chromium is a trace mineral required for insulin action and is often promoted for weight loss. Well-designed studies using up to 1,000 µg/day of the mineral do not show a significant effect on weight loss. A UL has not yet been determined for chromium, but some studies reported potentially serious side effects and, therefore, caution should be used when consuming more than 200 µg per day. While this supplement appears ineffective for weight loss, limited data suggest a potential for blood glucose improvements in people with type 2 diabetes. The key here is that chromium may be beneficial only in conjunction with weight management, carbohydrate control, and physical activity, not as a substitute for these lifestyle modifications.

❑ Pyruvate

Pyruvate is the end product of glycolysis and is often promoted for weight loss. Research is limited, but a few studies show a small effect on weight loss when large doses of pyruvate are ingested, usually in combination with large doses of the compound dihydroxyacetone (DHA). Common doses of pyruvate generally rage from 1-3 g/day, whereas the research studies used up to 30 g/day with up to 75 g of DHA. Taking these doses would be quite expensive. Data are insufficient to report on the safety of this supplement.

❑ Chitosan

Proponents for chitosan claim that it binds to dietary fat in the intestine and, thus, prevent fats absorption. Only a few published studies that used this product reported small differences in weight loss. Since the product is supposed to bind to fat in the digestive tract and eliminate it, it would follow that an increase in fecal fat would occur. Interestingly, one study examined fecal fat with use of chitosan and found it to be clinically insignificant in men and nonexistent in women. Some gastrointestinal side effects have been reported, such as flatulence, nausea, vomiting, and diarrhea.

❑ Conjugated Linoleic Acid

The compound conjugated linoleic acid (CLA) has several isomers, and it is believed that the two with the most biological activity are cis-9, trans-11 and trans-10, cis-12. Quite a few animal studies published report positive effects of CLA supplementation on fat loss and reduced energy consumption. It does seem that different species respond best to different isomers. However, some side effects have been seen in the animal studies such as insulin resistance and increased liver and spleen weight. The data in humans are not as promising, and not enough data exist to support its use for fat loss. More data are needed on appropriate isomers and doses in humans.

❑ Hydroxycitric Acid

Manufacturers of the supplement hydoxycitric acid (HCA) claim it is a stimulant and inhibits lipogenesis. A few animal studies have shown decreased food intake and weight regain after weight loss. The few studies in humans have mixed results; some studies showed small effects on weight loss while others showed none. More data are needed before conclusions can be made about the safety and efficacy of this product.

❑ Tea

The media promotion of green tea for weight loss has increased. It is believed that the active compounds in some teas—the powerful antioxidant epigallocatechin gallate (EGCG) and caffeine—may act to promote weight loss. Studies have been completed mostly with green and oolong teas, and some suggest small increases in fat oxidation, energy expenditure, and weight loss with consumption. These positive data are still sparse and should be interpreted with caution. It is important to understand that for people who are very sensitive to caffeine, consuming excessive amounts of tea can result in side effects. In addition, caffeine in high doses may be a banned substance for competitive athletes by their governing organization.

❑ Ma Huang/Ephedra/Ephedrine

Ma huang (also known as ephedra or ephedrine) was banned for sale in the United States by the Federal Drug Administration (FDA) in April 2004. Rigorous reviews of research studies do report modest increases in short-term weight loss with this product. However, the potential psychiatric, autonomic, and cardiac side effects were significant. It is important to emphasize that the possible small increases in weight loss are not worth the potential side effects of using the product, which may still be available for purchase in other countries.

❑ Citrus Aurantium

Now that ephedra/ephedrine products have been banned, citrus aurantium (CA) is a common ingredient in weight-loss products that claim to be "ephedra free" or "ephedrine free." It is also known as bitter orange or sour orange. The plant extract contains m-synephrine and phenylephrine, and it is believed that these are the active, stimulatory ingredients that aid in weight loss. The research on this compound is very scarce, and the few studies that have been done combined CA with ephedra/ephedrine, St. John's Wort, and/or caffeine, with one of these studies reporting greater weight loss with the product. The following question remains: Is it the CA itself or the CA acting with other compounds that results in the small increases in weight loss? Two studies did report a possible association between CA and cardiovascular side effects. More data are needed on this product before its efficacy or safety can be discussed with confidence.

❏ Calcium and Weight Loss

Media promotion of dairy foods for weight loss has increased and, therefore, understanding this relationship is important. One theory behind calcium and weight loss is as follows: Low calcium intake is associated with activation of vitamin D (1, 25-dihydroxyvitamin D), which in turn increases calcium deposition into the adipose tissue and pancreatic cells. When calcium concentrations increase in these cells, it promotes fatty acid synthesis and inhibits breakdown. Consuming adequate calcium would prevent these cellular changes and have the opposite effect on lipid metabolism. This theory is not a fact, which must be clearly explained to those interested in dairy products for weight loss.

Several epidemiological studies have examined the relationship between calcium intake and body weight and/or body fat and reported a negative association between the two variables. In the studies, groups of people who had lower calcium intakes have higher body weights than groups who consumed adequate or higher calcium. In addition to the population studies, two clinical trials have been published examining calcium intake and weight loss. One study concluded that three dairy servings a day resulted in more total and abdominal fat loss than calcium in the supplemental form or little daily intake of dairy products. All three groups were in a 500 kcal/day energy-restricted state. Another study reported that those eating three servings of yogurt per day, compared to a control group, experienced significantly more total fat loss and trunk fat loss.

Losing and keeping off weight takes hard work and dedication—
a message that consumers may not want to hear.

These data are probably not strong enough to make recommendations for all individuals. If people enjoy eating low- or non-fat dairy products as part of a healthy plan, the research data should be shared with them and they should be encouraged to continue to consume the products.

Summary

Overweight and obesity are conditions associated with an increased risk of many chronic diseases and medical complications. Both genetic and environmental factors are related to body weight and body fat. While genetic factors cannot be controlled, environmental factors can be. Two of the key environmental factors that influence body weight are food intake and physical activity. As a fitness professional, it is important to discuss the role of energy balance in weight management.

Sound weight-management plans include controlling energy intake and regular physical activity in such a way to induce lifelong changes in habits. Hundreds of fad diets and plans are available and yet, oftentimes, very little scientific evidence exists to support their use. It is important to use knowledge of physiology when evaluating the claims. However, some practical books and plans that teach the sound principles of weight management are available. People who lose weight may have difficulty actually keeping it off, and it is important to guide clients toward those sound plans to encourage lifelong success.

Many weight-loss supplements are on the market, with most promising amazing results. Unfortunately, data do not support the efficacy of many products and limited research data are available on some of the others, so that no firm conclusions about their safety and efficacy can be made. Less is known about long-term safety.

The data available suggests that to lose weight and keep it off, the two key factors are controlled energy intake and regular physical activity. Losing and keeping off weight takes hard work and dedication—a message that consumers may not want to hear. People may want to purchase a magic pill and watch the pounds melt away. It is important to acknowledge the hard work it takes to maintain energy balance, but, at the same time, promote and share the tools needed to succeed and provide critical motivation and support. Obesity would not be the epidemic that it is today if losing and maintaining weight were as easy as some diets and supplements promise.

13

Disordered Eating

Being considerably underweight, severely restricting food, or regularly binging and purging are symptoms indicative of the classically known eating disorders anorexia nervosa (AN) and bulimia nervosa (BN). However, it may be that an individual does not have the obvious symptoms of these disorders. When someone says "I never eat dessert," "I think about food all the time," or "I have to exercise several hours per week to maintain my weight," it is possible that he has some type of an eating-related problem. These behaviors may fall into a newly recognized set of symptoms referred to as disordered eating (DE).

While no one common definition for normal eating exists, it is generally characterized by the following: eating when hungry until gently satisfied; choosing a majority of foods that are considered healthy, while using moderate restraint with total energy intake and consumption of unhealthier foods; and allowing for regular planning, but with flexibility, not rigidity. In this chapter, eating disorders and DE will be distinguished, and suggestions for working with individuals who fall into these categories will be discussed.

Eating Disorders

Several eating disorders diagnoses are based on strict criteria set by the Diagnostic and Statistical Manual of Psychiatric Disorders (DSM-IV). These psychiatric conditions have the common theme of issues and preoccupation with body image. A brief overview of these conditions is presented in the following sections.

❑ Anorexia Nervosa

AN is characterized by an intense fear of becoming fat and a refusal to maintain a healthy body weight. The restricting type of AN is associated with self-starvation and excessive exercise. People with the binge-eating/purging type participate in self-starvation and excessive exercise, but occasionally binge and compensate with an inappropriate behavior, such as vomiting or laxative abuse. While the prevalence of all eating disorders is hard to quantify because not all individuals affected will seek medical help and some may not meet the strict criteria for diagnosis, it is estimated that approximately 0.5-1.0% of the population may have this disorder. While AN is more common in females, it can affect males as well.

❑ Bulimia Nervosa

BN is characterized by consuming large quantities of food (binging) followed by a compensatory behavior to prevent body-weight gain. BN of the purging type is associated with compensatory behaviors such as vomiting or using laxatives, diuretics, or enemas, while the behaviors associated with the nonpurging type are fasting or excessive exercise. Since people with BN may be of normal body weight, it is important to look for other signs and symptoms such as eroded teeth (due to stomach acid) or scars on the hands (due to using the fingers to induce vomiting).

❑ Eating Disorders Not Otherwise Specified

This third category of eating disorders, eating disorders not otherwise specified (EDNOS), is defined in the DSM-IV, but the criteria are not as specific as those listed for AN or BN. EDNOS was created to identify individuals who do not meet all specifications, but have some of the individual criteria for AN or BN. Examples of some of the EDNOS include the following:
- Basic characteristics for AN, except there is regular menses or the body weight is low but within the normal range
- Basic characteristics of BN are met, except the person may not vomit as frequently as required in the criteria, may vomit after a normal-sized meal, or may not swallow chewed food
- Binge eating disorder: a condition where a person repeatedly binges on food but does not exhibit the compensatory behavior to avoid weight gain

❑ Anorexia Athletica

While not an official eating disorder listed in the DSM-IV, anorexia athletica is common in athletes who use energy restriction and/or excessive exercise to maintain a low body weight in an attempt to enhance performance. Individuals may not have a distorted body image but have the belief that a certain body weight or composition will give a competitive edge.

❑ Muscle Dysmorphia

Unlike the other conditions listed here, muscle dysmorphia is more likely to occur in males and is characterized by preoccupation with becoming lean and muscular. This disorder may coexist with other conditions such as obsessive-compulsive disorder, depression, eating disorder characteristics or behaviors, or use and abuse of pharmacological agents to induce muscle growth. The incidence and prevalence of muscle dysmorphia is not well known, as it has not yet been well studied.

❑ Female Athlete Triad

The term female athlete triad is used to bring together three related conditions of DE (usually a low energy intake), amenorrhea, and osteopenia or osteoporosis (low bone density). The condition can occur in any female athlete, but appears to be more likely in sports that emphasize leanness. The American College of Sports Medicine (ACSM) has published an updated Position Stand on the topic titled "The Female Athlete Triad" (www.acsm.org). The female athlete triad is treated the same way as other eating disorders or DE patterns.

Jupiterimages

The female athlete triad is treated the same way as other eating disorders or DE patterns.

Eating Disorders Information

In addition to ACSM's Position Stand and current nutrition text books, a valuable resource for any health professional is the National Eating Disorders Association website (www.nationaleatingdisorders.org). Examples of the information that is available from the organization include the following:

- Background information, definitions, and characteristics of the different types of eating disorders
- Physiological complications of eating disorders
- Issues relating to healthy body image
- Prevention of eating disorders
- Helping a person with eating disorders
- Seeking treatment

Some of the information from this organization is included in the following sections.

Physiological Consequences of Eating Disorders

Many physiological consequences result from eating disorders and DE. The magnitude of the consequences depends on the severity of the disorder or condition. The National Eating Disorders Association has summarized the health consequences of AN and BN (refer to Appendix E1).

The Treatment Team

The terms eating disorders or DE may be misleading when discussing treatment options because the names imply that the solution would be to simply learn how to eat normally. On the contrary, these conditions represent a collection of complex socio-cultural, psychological, and physiological issues. It is important to ultimately refer a person who may have an eating disorder to a member of an interdisciplinary team of health professionals with expertise in this area. In institutions, such as college campuses and healthcare facilities, the treatment team usually includes a physician, registered dietitian, and psychologist or psychiatrist, with each team member having unique knowledge and skills to optimize patient recovery. The primary objectives of the treatment team are to help the individual identify and cope with the emotional problems that lead to the DE, alter the destructive thought processes that sustain the DE, and normalize body image and eating behaviors.

How Can the Fitness Professional Help?

Of all the team members, the fitness professional may be the frontline person in recognizing a person who needs professional help. The fitness professional may have most regular contact with the client and already have an established, trusted relationship. Unfortunately, the fitness professional is typically not included in the treatment team. The National Eating Disorders Association encourages fitness professionals to recognize the signs and symptoms of eating disorders, understand the potential effects, actively discourage dangerous exercise practices in an attempt to control weight, and encourage a positive self-image.

While it is not the fitness professional's responsibility to initiate and provide the psychological, medical, or nutritional therapy needed for treatment, it is important to be knowledgeable about community resources to which clients can be referred. The registered dietitian should provide the medical nutrition therapy and help establish a regular pattern of eating. The fitness professional should work with the dietitian and the treatment team to do the following:

- Help the individual understand the concept of healthy body weight and body composition and to help him achieve and maintain a body weight that is healthy and appropriate.
- Emphasize that a lower body weight or body-fat percentage will not always enhance performance.
- Discourage the idea that a certain body size or composition will automatically lead to a happier life.
- Help the individual set safe, realistic exercise goals.
- Emphasize exercise for the health benefits, the joy of feeling the body move, and, possibly, increased strength, and that it is not just a means for burning off calories.
- Be a role model of healthy self-esteem and body-image. Base self-value on goals, accomplishments, talents, and personality rather than on body composition.
- Offer to be available to the other members of the treatment team.

Jupiterimages

While it is not the fitness professional's responsibility to initiate and provide the psychological, medical, or nutritional therapy needed for treatment of eating disorders and disordered eating, it is important to be knowledgeable about community resources to which clients can be referred.

If it is suspected that an individual has a problem, gently encourage that trained professional help is sought. The National Eating Disorders Association offers several guidelines for approaching and helping a person suffering from DE or eating disorders and some of these are presented in Appendices E2 through E6. Two of the sets of recommendations were designed for educators working with students (Appendices E2 and E3). The fitness professional can replace the term "student" with "client," and the information is very practical and applicable to many people. Another recommendation set refers to helping a friend (Appendix E4) and another set presents what should be said if an eating disorder is suspected (Appendix E5). Use these guidelines when working with a friend, family member, or client. Detailed information on seeking treatment is also available from this the National Eating Disorders Association.

Summary

While eating disorders are medically defined, many people can exhibit DE patterns. Because of the physical and psychological consequences associated with these conditions, identification and referral for treatment are essential to ensure optimal health for clients who may be at risk. Fitness professionals should possess a working knowledge of the risk factors and warning signs of DE and be familiar with available local treatment programs. As part of the multidisciplinary approach to treatment, fitness professionals can assist by emphasizing a healthy body weight and image and recommending an appropriate amount of exercise consistent with good health.

ANSWERS TO COMMONLY ASKED QUESTIONS

Part III

Hemera/Thinkstock

As a fitness professional, it is important to be able to discuss certain issues and answer certain types of nutrition questions. The purpose of this section is to serve as a guide to answering these questions, while staying within the scope of the fitness professional's expertise. While the questions posed in this section are not all-inclusive, they do reflect some common topics that clients may want to know more about.

❑ If the *Dietary Guidelines* and MyPyramid are accurate, why is there an obesity problem in America?

The best answer to this question is that only a small percentage of the American population actually follows the guidelines. Many people consume excess energy and are physically inactive. The current guidelines are designed to address obesity and chronic disease.

❑ How much of each nutrient does a person need?

Refer to the Dietary Reference Intakes (DRIs). This is a collaborative effort between the Food and Nutrition Board of the Institute of Medicine in the United States and Health Canada. DRIs are designed to meet the needs of approximately 97-98% of the healthy population. These recommendations may not be valid if a person has a disease or medical condition. Free copies of the DRIs can be downloaded from the USDA website (www.usda.gov) and can be found in Appendix C2.

❑ Why are dietary guidelines always changing? Why can't health professionals make up their minds?

It has nothing to do with health processionals changing their minds. Dietary guidelines change as a result of newly available research data. Whenever a dietary guideline is released, it is based on the data available at the time. As more research is conducted and published, increased evidence exists to strengthen the recommendations.

❑ Why is it that many nutrition-related claims seem important today, but are gone in six months?

Often the media will report the results of a single research study as fact. Sometimes the person reporting does not pay attention to the study size or the statistical or clinical significance. A media headline is not the same as a government-issued dietary guideline or an abundance of scientific evidence.

❑ How many calories does a person need?

Several ways of estimating energy expenditure are available. One method is a simple chart based on age, weight, and gender, while the other is a more complicated equation. Both methods provide estimates, but are good starting points. Actual energy needs may differ. If a person is consuming exactly the "required" amount of calories but is still gaining weight, then that estimated value is too high and needs to be adjusted.

❑ If someone follows the MyPryamid plan precisely, what would prevent him from losing weight?

First, the meal plan needs to include an energy deficit. If this is not specified, the plan will be created for weight maintenance. Second, the energy needs and meal plan that are presented on MyPyramid are just an estimate. They provide a good starting point, but may need to be adjusted by the user. Third, consumers tend to underreport their serving sizes and total food intake. Underreporting is not usually purposeful, just a misunderstanding of portion sizes. People need to measure portion sizes at first and then can move away from this process once they become more proficient in judging portion sizes accurately. Estimating portion sizes gets easier when the same dishes are used (e.g., the same cereal bowl each morning). Finally, people do not always count items like hard candies, gum, small handfuls of snacks, or beverages. Depending on the state in which a fitness professional works, it may not be appropriate to conduct a nutrition assessment on a client. It is appropriate, however, to encourage the client to record and consume accurate portions, watch for hidden calories, and examine the role of physical activity in his energy balance equation.

❑ What is the difference between foods that are enriched versus those that are fortified?

When grains are processed, many of the nutrients are lost. Enrichment is the process of adding back some of the nutrients lost with processing. Fortification is when a nutrient is added to a food that does not normally contain it. Examples are calcium-fortified orange juice or soy milk.

❑ What is the difference between whole wheat and whole grain?

Whole grains are grains that are not refined—they are milled in their complete form with only the husk removed. Wheat flour is any flour made from wheat and may include unbleached flour or white flour. Whole-wheat bread, for example, may be brown in color due to lack of bleaching, but the fiber content may vary. To maximize fiber content in a product, look for the terms "whole grain" on the label.

❑ Are carbohydrates bad?

First, carbohydrate (glucose) is necessary for the brain and other organs to function properly. If blood glucose falls too low, a coma can result. Carbohydrates also fuel the working muscle during exercise, with more fuel coming from carbohydrate as exercise intensity increases. Without adequate carbohydrate, exercise performance will suffer. It is important to explain the role of carbohydrate in fueling the skeletal muscle and organs.

Second, different qualities of carbohydrate are available. Many carbohydrate-rich foods (e.g., fruits, vegetables, and whole grains) contain fiber, vitamins, minerals, antioxidants, and phytochemicals. Eliminating these foods from the diet is not prudent for good health.

Carbohydrates will cause fat gain if more are eaten than are stored as glycogen or burned as fuel. Carbohydrates consumed in proper quantities will not promote weight gain. Think about elite distance runners—are they fat? No, even though they do consume large quantities of carbohydrate. Many sedentary individuals consume all macronutrients in excess, which leads to a positive energy balance and weight gain.

Insulin has been labeled by some as an undesirable anabolic hormone that promotes fat storage. It is true that it is anabolic, but it also plays a role in skeletal muscle protein synthesis. Insulin will promote fat storage if more carbohydrate is consumed than the body needs to replenish glycogen stores or use as fuel. If normal quantities of carbohydrate are eaten, the insulin response is not an important issue.

❏ What is the relationship between oat fiber and lower cholesterol levels?

Commercials on television promote consumption of oat fiber to reduce serum cholesterol. Scientific data do support this claim—in fact, an FDA-approved health claim exists for the relationship (www.fda.gov). A key theory behind this observation involves the behavior of soluble fiber in the gastrointestinal tract. The soluble fiber acts as a sponge by absorbing some dietary fat consumed with a meal and by absorbing bile (a compound made in the liver and stored in the gallbladder that aids digestion). This filled sponge-like substance is not digested in the small intestine and is ultimately excreted by the body. As it is excreted, the fat and bile go with it. Under normal circumstances, bile in the small intestine is recycled and reused. Since some is lost with the excretion of fiber, the body needs to make more. A key compound needed for bile synthesis is cholesterol. The liver can get some cholesterol to make more bile from the bloodstream. This theory explains how blood cholesterol drops in response to regular consumption of oat fiber.

❏ Why do some people supplement with B vitamins to prevent heart disease?

This new area of research has to do with the compound homocysteine. Homocysteine is an intermediate in normal protein metabolism and the vitamins B6, B12, and folate play an important role in keeping this metabolic intermediate from building up. It is believed that high levels of homocysteine may cause arterial damage and, thus, contribute to the atherogenesis process. If a person is supplementing for this reason, it is important that he discuss this with his physician.

❏ Why do people take niacin to lower cholesterol?

Niacin is a B vitamin that when taken in pharmacological doses (>50 mg/day) may lower levels of low-density lipoprotein (LDL) and increase levels of high-density lipoprotein (HDL). Due to the media reporting of this research, many people are taking niacin for this purpose. The UL for niacin is 35 mg per day, but many people are taking a gram or more. Unfortunately, though niacin may improve blood lipids, it may also cause liver problems and other undesirable side effects. If a person is taking supplemental niacin to control blood lipids, it is important to discuss this with his physician.

❏ Are artificial sweeteners bad?

This question is tough to answer because of the vagueness of the term "bad." Artificial sweeteners are classified by the FDA as food additives (www.fda.gov). Similar to drugs, food additives must undergo years of testing before they are approved for use. Currently, all of the artificial sweeteners sold legally in the United States are approved for sale and use. The key word here is "artificial." These products are chemicals; however, their safety has been tested. It is probably best not to encourage or discourage use of these products, but instead explain the strict regulation that food additives must undergo and then let the individual make the decision whether or not to use the product.

❏ Where do ketones come from and are they good for weight loss?

Everybody makes ketones, but production increases with the consumption of low-carbohydrate diets. Carbohydrates are needed for the complete oxidation of a fatty acid molecule. If carbohydrate is limited, the normal pathway for fat breakdown is altered, and another pathway is available. The end product of this alternate pathway causes ketone production. Ketones are acids that alter the pH of the body when large amounts are accumulated. When people consume low-carbohydrate diets, enough ketones are produced to cause side effects, including bad breath and appetite suppression, but generally people do not end up with a severe medical condition called ketoacidosis. In short, ketones come from the incomplete breakdown of fatty acids.

❏ Why do people with diabetes sometimes develop ketoacidosis?

Ketoacidosis is common in people with uncontrolled type 1 diabetes. These individuals have plenty of carbohydrate (glucose) in the blood, but the glucose cannot enter the cells without insulin. As a result, the cells try to rely on fat for fuel, but fatty acids cannot be completely oxidized without carbohydrate and therefore ketones form. In this case, the levels can build up to the point where a person's body becomes so acidic that he can end up in a coma and die. This condition is serious and requires medical attention.

❏ If a protein product has a biological value (BV) greater than 100%, is it superior to food?

Biological value compares the amount of nitrogen absorbed from the diet with that retained in body for maintenance and growth. Egg has a BV of 100%, meaning that 100% of the nitrogen that is absorbed is retained.

Many protein products are quite expensive, while foods like eggs and milk are not. Products that have a BV greater than 100% are not absolutely necessary—foods can still provide the body with all of the needed amino acids. If a person is worried that food has a lower BV than the newest supplement, taking an extra few bites of chicken or a few extra gulps of milk should compensate.

❑ Is whey protein the best form of protein?

While a few studies have suggested that consumption of the branched-chain amino acids (leucine, isoleucine, and valine) aid in the postexercise protein synthesis process, insufficient evidence exists to conclude that any particular type of protein is superior to others. Whey protein supplements get much attention due to their leucine content. Other foods are also good sources of leucine, including milk, tuna, and cottage cheese.

❑ If too much protein is consumed, isn't the excess excreted in the urine?

Any amino acid that is not being used for protein synthesis, glucose synthesis, or ATP production is converted to a fatty acid and stored in the adipose tissue. In this process it is true that the nitrogen from the amino acid will get converted to urea and excreted, but the carbon skeleton is not destroyed and is used to make a fatty acid. Consuming too many calories will result in body fat gain, even if the extra calories are in the form of protein.

❑ Will consuming too much protein put too much stress on the kidneys?

It is true that the kidney must handle the nitrogen/urea from excess protein intake; however, it is not clear if this is a problem in people with healthy kidneys. People with renal disease cannot handle too much protein; but, this may not be the same case for healthy people. Until more research data are available, a confident answer to this question cannot be given. A lack of research data does not imply or guarantee safety.

❑ Are protein needs met for a person who is practicing a vegan diet?

People who choose vegan diets consume no animal products, which are complete proteins. If a person who is a vegan consumes soy or has a wide variety of plant foods in the diet, it is possible to meet protein needs. Incomplete proteins (most plants) lack one or more essential amino acids, but can be combined to provide all of the essential ones (e.g., by combining rice and beans). The complementary foods do not have to be consumed in the same meal to get the benefits; a person can consume these foods throughout the day.

❑ Do all people need to drink eight, 8-ounce glasses of water per day?

It is not clear where this "8 by 8" rule came from. While this recommendation may be appropriate for some people, fluid needs also depend on physical-activity levels, environment, and sweat rate. Fluid recommendations also differ before, during, and after exercise. Refer to the American College of Sports Medicine Position Stand "Exercise and Fluid Replacement" for details (www.acsm.org).

❑ Do fluid requirements need to be met with plain water or do all fluids count?

All fluids count toward the daily need, including water found in foods. Consuming all types of beverages, regardless of their sugar or caffeine content, will contribute to fluid needs.

❑ Won't caffeinated beverages dehydrate?

While caffeine may be a diuretic, the current evidence suggests that it will not lead to dehydration as long as total fluid needs are met. Refer to the American College of Sports Medicine Position Stand "Exercise and Fluid Replacement" for details (www.acsm.org).

❑ Is it better to consume a sports drink or water?

If a person is exercising at low or moderate intensity for 30-45 minutes, plain water is fine. Sports drinks are designed to replace the carbohydrate and electrolytes lost with higher exercise intensities that are continuous and last longer than 45-60 minutes or are intermittent in nature. A warm environment may also increase fluid and electrolyte needs and a sports drink may be appropriate in this situation.

❑ Are commercial sports drink needed or can they be made?

Commercial sports drinks are formulated to replace the carbohydrate and electrolytes lost with exercise and these formulas are based on abundant scientific research. The products are readily available and inexpensive, especially in the powdered form. If a person is completely against using a commercial sports drink, he could attempt to mimic the formula by mixing one cup of orange juice (or other juice with potassium) with one cup of water and adding 1/8 teaspoon of salt. This beverage will not contain the ideal mixture of carbohydrate sources (fructose, glucose, sucrose, glucose polymers) and the fructose alone in the juice may cause gastrointestinal stress.

❑ Are fitness waters necessary? What are the benefits?

Fitness waters are lower in electrolytes and carbohydrate (3 g per cup) than traditional sports drinks (14-15 g per cup). Research supports increased fluid intake when the beverage tastes good. Some people need the fluid because they are exercising in a warm environment, but are not exercising intensely or long enough to warrant carbohydrate replacement. Fitness waters could be a desirable beverage in this situation. Caution should be used with excessive consumption if the water contains vitamins and minerals that have an upper limit established.

❑ Are vitamin waters and energy bars necessary?

Many people purchase foods and beverages with added vitamins, minerals, and/or herbs not only for the calories, but because of the perceived benefit of consuming these foods. Many fortified products exist on the market today, from waters, to bars, to whole foods. If a person is consuming more than the upper limit for a nutrient (see the DRIs presented in Appendix C2), toxicity symptoms may result. Many people who consume fortified foods also may be taking vitamin and mineral supplements. In some states, it is inappropriate to conduct a nutrition assessment and quantify their intake. It is important to educate people about the DRIs and have them examine if they really need to be consuming the fortified products in question.

❑ Will taking a vitamin and mineral supplement enhance performance?

If a person is not deficient in a vitamin or mineral, taking more will not enhance performance. While exercise may slightly increase the need for a few vitamins and minerals, the increased needs are small and can be met with the extra calories needed to support training.

❑ Does exercise increase the production of free radicals?

Free radicals are molecules that are thought to cause cellular damage. Antioxidant nutrients neutralize these free radicals in the body and are, therefore, recommended in the diet. Exercise will increase free radical production, but it also induces the synthesis of the body's antioxidant enzymes. It is believed that exercise does not contribute to the free-radical-induced damage thought to play a role in aging or chronic disease.

❑ Can anybody change his body shape with appropriate nutrition and exercise?

While all nutrition and fitness professionals agree that proper nutrition and exercise are important for maintaining a healthy body composition, not everybody can significantly alter his body shape. Genetics plays a large role in body types. Some individuals, who are tall and lean, may never have the physique of a competitive bodybuilder. Similarly, individuals who are naturally larger may never be able to "diet" or train enough to become an elite marathon runner. It is important to help clients achieve a healthy body composition while encouraging realistic goals. Genetics should not be an excuse to avoid exercise.

❑ How is weight gained?

Most people asking this question are looking to increase muscle mass, not gain body fat. In order to gain muscle a person must have a positive energy balance and perform resistance training. Generally, an additional 400-500 kcals/day are needed, including adequate protein for strength training (1.5-2.0 g/kg).

❏ Will eating several smaller meals in a day stimulate my metabolism?

There is some scientific data supporting the idea that multiple smaller meals spread throughout the day are better than two or three larger meals because the smaller meals "keep the furnace burning" or, more technically, increase the thermic effect of food. The magnitude of the additional calories burned is not very high (i.e., maybe 25 calories per day). Though the value may be small, it can add up over a period of time.

Smaller meals may contribute to successful weight loss and maintenance in another way. If a long period of time passes between meals, blood glucose levels may drop, which triggers fatigue and hunger. This physiologically driven hunger may result in overeating at the next meal. By keeping blood glucose level throughout the day, the highs and lows of blood sugar can be prevented and hunger better controlled.

❏ Does metabolism slow down with age?

Research data suggest that as people age, a significant loss of skeletal muscle mass takes place due to physical inactivity. Unfortunately, resting metabolic rate may also decline in proportion to the muscle mass loss. The good news is that several research studies have reported that previously sedentary older adults respond well to resistance training and are capable of increasing both strength and muscle mass. Encouraging people to maintain muscle mass throughout life is the ideal strategy, but working with previously sedentary older clients is also warranted.

❏ Will eating at certain times of the day promote weight gain?

Many diet plans will make recommendations that include no consumption of carbohydrates past 3:00 p.m. or no food at all past 7:00 p.m. This issue can be examined in two ways. From a physiological and digestive standpoint, the body does not know what time it is. Food can be digested with the same efficiency in the morning as in the evening. One of the claims in support of this idea is that eating before bed leads the food to be stored as fat. This is true, but the whole picture needs to be examined. The body is chronically storing fat in the adipose tissue and breaking it down when needed. In other words, just because a meal is stored as fat does not mean that it will remain in the adipose tissue forever. If a large evening meal is consumed and then used for fuel during a morning workout, it will not contribute to significant weight gain in the long term. If that large evening meal is not used for fuel, it may contribute to permanent body fat mass. The main concern here is long-term energy balance over several days, not just in a 12-hour period.

Another factor that is valid about meal timing has to do with behavior. If a person who is trying to lose weight skips meals, he may often end up excessively hungry in the evening, which could trigger the consumption of an enormous dinner. In this case, it is better to balance out food intake throughout the day to prevent overeating at one meal.

Finally, many occupations involve people working evening shifts. If a person gets off work at 11:00 p.m. or 3:00 a.m., is he supposed to not eat? As long as energy balance is maintained over the long term, the actual time of day does not matter.

❑ Do the calories from beverages need to be counted?

Yes! It is important to point this fact out to clients. Many popular smoothie shops and coffee houses offer drinks that can have several hundred calories. In addition, a can of soda has an average of 150 calories. Many people do not think about this since it is just a beverage and not a chewable food.

❑ How can the status of bone health be determined?

When people go for a physical exam, often physicians will order blood work. While this practice is very useful in determining disease risk or diagnosing many diseases, it is not helpful for measuring bone health. While approximately 99% of the body's calcium is in bone, the remainder is in the blood and is essential for muscle contraction. Serum calcium is maintained within a very narrow window. If it drops just a bit, muscle contraction (e.g., heart beat) can be disrupted. When serum calcium drops, the calcium from bone can be used to restore the normal level. If a person's endocrine system is working properly, serum calcium will always be normal. The best way to evaluate the density of bones is through Dual-energy x-ray absorptiometry (DXA or DEXA). This procedure usually requires a physician's order.

❑ Are people genetically destined to be overweight or obese?

Genetics plays a large role in overweight and obesity. American society implies that ultrathin is the norm. Some people, no matter how much they control their food intake and exercise, will never be thin, and this is perfectly acceptable. However, people should not use the excuse of a family history of obesity to give up and not even bother to live a healthy lifestyle. For example, if a female client 5'4" tall, weighs 220 lb, and has obese parents, it is hard to determine whether her obesity is due to lifestyle or genetics, but at the same time this is not that important. This person may never weigh the "ideal" 120 lb due to genetic factors. However, with lifestyle modification, she may be able to weigh 150 or 160 lb. It is important to work with clients and to determine a healthy body weight for them and to focus on fitness.

❑ Why do some people on high animal-fat diets lower their cholesterol levels?

If people follow a low-carbohydrate, high-fat diet properly, they will lose some weight because such diets generally are low in calories. When a person loses weight, serum cholesterol levels will generally drop, no matter how the weight was lost. Limited research data are available examining the long-term effects of low-carbohydrate, high animal-fat diets on blood lipids or incidence of heart disease.

❏ How much exercise is necessary for weight loss and weight maintenance?

The amount of exercise necessary for weight loss and weight maintenance is more than that recommended for good health. Data from the National Weight Control Registry, a large research trial examining successful weight loss and maintenance, indicate that 90% of the successful members exercise about one hour per day. The women had an average weekly energy expenditure of approximately 2,500 calories, while the men expended approximately 3,900 calories. Other data suggest that 60-90 minutes per day of accumulated physical activity is necessary for weight maintenance, with an energy expenditure goal of at least 2,000 calories per week. It is important to work with individuals to help them find activities that they will perform on a regular basis.

❏ If an individual reduces the risk factors for disease, is he then safe?

Many health campaigns promote knowing personal numbers. This advice may apply to blood lipids, blood pressure, or blood glucose. It is important to understand the relationship between risk factors and disease development. For example, dyslipidemia is a risk factor for developing cardiovascular disease and hypertension is a risk factor for having a stroke. However, people with normal blood lipids or blood pressures can develop these conditions. Having positive risk factors significantly increases the likelihood of developing disease, but not having those risk factors does not preclude a person from ever getting a particular disease.

❏ How much weight loss is needed to see health benefits?

Some overweight and obese people believe that they must achieve some unrealistic, "ideal" body weight in order to receive any health benefits. Fortunately, many people with chronic disease symptoms, such as elevated blood lipids, blood glucose, or blood pressure, can see improvements with modest weight loss of approximately 10% of body weight. Use this information to encourage individuals to make those small steps toward improving health.

❏ What is the fitness professionals' role in the treatment of eating disorders?

Eating disorders represent a collection of complex socio-cultural, psychological, and physiological issues that require treatment from an interdisciplinary team of health professionals with expertise in this area. A person suspected of having an eating disorder should ultimately be referred to a qualified health professional. The National Eating Disorders Association (www.nationaleatingdisorders.org) is an organization that provides a wealth of resources for both lay individuals and health professionals. Many resources are available for help with approaching individuals who display behaviors consistent with an eating problem. Some of these resources are presented in Appendices E1 through E6 of this book. It is important for a fitness professional to play a role in the treatment team because of the regular contact with the person and the trusted relationship that may have been established. The important word here is team—people with eating disorders need help from physicians, psychiatrists or psychologists, registered dietitians, and fitness professionals. Do not attempt to treat anybody with disordered eating symptoms without input from other appropriate allied health professionals.

❑ Does a person burn more fat when exercising at low intensity?

During low-intensity exercise, a greater percentage of the total calories come from fat. However, more total fat calories can be burned by higher-intensity exercise. When two, 20-minute exercise bouts are compared, one at lower intensity and one at higher intensity, the lower intensity bout expends 100 calories—80% from fat (i.e., 80 fat calories). At the higher intensity, 200 calories are burned and only 50% are from fat, or 100 fat calories. If time is not a factor, a person could exercise for a longer duration at the lower intensity and burn the same number of total fat calories. On the other hand, lower-intensity exercise does not provide the same degree of cardiovascular benefits as moderate- or high-intensity exercise.

❑ What is the difference between glycemic index and glycemic load?

Glycemic index (GI) is defined as the incremental area under the plasma glucose curve in response to 50 g of available carbohydrate, in the fasted state, as compared to a reference food (glucose or white bread). In simple terms, it is a rating scale of a food's potential to raise blood glucose levels. A food with a "high" GI may cause large fluctuations in blood glucose. Initially, a large rise in blood glucose may occur, followed by a large increase in insulin secretion, which then may result in a dramatic fall in blood glucose concentrations.

Glycemic load (GL) is the amount of total carbohydrate in a food multiplied by the GI of the carbohydrate in that food. A normal portion of food may have a high GI, but a low GL.

❑ Is it better to use glycemic index or glycemic load?

Either method should be used as a tool, not a rule. This information is useful if the body needs glucose quickly. In this case, choosing a high-GI food or product is appropriate. However, the GI should not always be a rule, especially when people believe they need to avoid certain foods. For example, carrots have a relatively high GI (~68) for a vegetable, but the GL is approximately 3.

Teaching clients the limitations of GI and GL and encouraging them to know their own body response is important.

❑ Are there other factors that affect the glycemic index of a food?

Many factors may affect the GI of a food. Examples include the following: changes in particle size (e.g., mashing a potato); cooking; variety (e.g., a potato grown in Canada vs Idaho); maturation and ripening; addition of protein (e.g., adding chicken and cheese to a baked potato); and variability within foods (e.g., ice cream may have a GI of 35-65).

❏ What are functional foods?

Functional foods are those that provide health benefits because of the compounds they contain beyond the traditional nutrients. For example, many fruits and vegetables contain phytochemicals, which are nonnutritive compounds with apparent health benefits.

❏ What are probiotics and prebiotics?

Probiotics are examples of functional foods that contain live microorganisms that occur naturally or are added to the food. Their purpose is to promote a positive bacterial environment in the intestines. Prebiotics are nondigestible fibers that promote the growth of the beneficial gut bacteria. Prebiotics may occur naturally or may be added to a food.

❏ What is exercise-induced hyponatremia and how can it be avoided?

Exercise-induced hyponatremia is a condition where plasma sodium falls to a level than can be dangerous. The most common cause of this condition is when a person loses significant amounts of sodium through sweat loss and replaces the lost fluid with plain water. This can be avoided by consuming appropriate amounts of fluid and sodium to match the amount lost in sweat. Many sports drinks and products are readily available and can be used to prevent this condition.

❏ Is drinking soda bad for the bones?

The mineral phosphorus is an important component of the hydroxyapatite found in bones (provides harness to bone tissue). Phosphorus is found in many common foods including milk, meats, and eggs. Phosphoric acid is found in many soft drinks. A few studies have suggested an association between soft drink consumption and reduced bone mass. The proposed theories for this association were the following:
- Consuming soft drinks in place of milk leads to a decreased calcium intake.
- The acid and phosphorus in the soft drinks results in increased calcium loss.
- Caffeine in soft drinks results in increased calcium loss.

More recent studies suggest that it is likely the inadequate calcium consumption rather than intake of phosphorus or caffeine that leads to reduced bone mass.

Appendices

iStockphoto/Thinkstock

Within these pages, you will find an assortment of tools that you can use when discussing nutrition with your clients. Appendices A through D include information about energy and nutrient intake. Appendices E and F provide guidelines on working with clients who may have an eating disorder. Be sure to visit the websites referred to within the appendices for updated information.

Appendix A1: Eating Healthier and Feeling Better
        Using the Nutrition Facts Label

Appendix A2: Working Together...*Dietary Guidelines*, Food Guidance System,
        Food Label

Appendix B1: Examples of FDA-Approved Nutrient Content Health Claims

Appendix B2: Examples of FDA-Approved Health Claims

Appendix C1: Vitamin and Mineral Table

Appendix C2: Dietary Reference Intakes (DRIs)

Appendix D1: MyPyramid Food Intake Patterns

Appendix D2: MyPyramid Food Intake Pattern Calorie Levels

Appendix E1: Health Consequences of Eating Disorders

Appendix E2: The Role of the Educator: Faculty and Student Guidelines
        for Meeting With and Referring Students Who May
        Have Eating Disorders

Appendix E3: The Role of the Educator: Some "Don'ts" for Educators and
        Others Concerned About a Person With an Eating Disorder

Appendix E4: How to Help a Friend With Eating and Body Image Issues

Appendix E5: What Should I Say? Tips for Talking to a Friend Who May Be
        Struggling With an Eating Disorder

Appendix E6: What Can You Do to Help Prevent Eating Disorders?

Appendix F: Finding Your Way to a Healthier You

Appendix A1

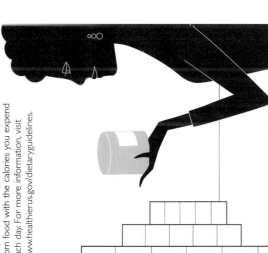

Eating healthier and
feeling better using the

Nutrition
Facts Label

U.S. Department of Health and Human Services
U.S. Department of Agriculture
www.healthierus.gov/dietaryguidelines

FDA is responsible for promoting and protecting the public's health by ensuring that the nation's food supply is safe, sanitary, wholesome, and honestly labeled.

August, 2006

HERE'S WHERE TO FIND MORE INFORMATION ON HEALTHY LIVING:

U.S. Department of Health and Human Services

Dietary Guidelines for Americans
www.healthierus.gov/dietaryguidelines

Dietary Approaches to Stop Hypertension (DASH)
www.nhlbi.nih.gov/health/public/heart/hbp/dash

U.S. Food and Drug Administration

Nutrition Facts Label
www.cfsan.fda.gov/~dms/foodlab.html

U.S. Centers for Disease Control and Prevention

Nutrition and Physical Activity
www.cdc.gov/nccdphp/dnpa

U.S. Department of Agriculture

Nutrition Information
www.nutrition.gov

Food Pyramid
www.mypyramid.gov

THE RIGHT TOOL TO BALANCE YOUR DIET

You probably already use the Nutrition Facts label in some way—maybe to check calories, fat or sodium content. But, the more familiar you are with the information, the more you'll want to use it daily to ensure you're eating a healthy, balanced diet.

Use the label when you shop, as you plan your meals, and as you cook each day. The label makes it easy to determine the amounts of nutrients you're getting and to compare one product to another.

Strive for a diet that emphasizes fruits, vegetables, whole grains, and fat-free or low-fat milk and milk products. Include lean meats, poultry, fish, beans, and nuts. Choose foods that are low in saturated fats, trans fats, cholesterol, salt, and added sugar.

Regular physical activity is important for your overall health and fitness. It also helps you control body weight by balancing the calories you take in from food with the calories you expend each day. For more information, visit www.healthierus.gov/dietaryguidelines.

USE THE NUTRITION FACTS LABEL TO EAT HEALTHIER

Check the serving size and number of servings.

- The Nutrition Facts Label information is based on ONE serving, but many packages contain more. Look at the serving size and how many servings you are actually consuming. If you double the servings you eat, you double the calories and nutrients, including the % DVs.

- When you compare calories and nutrients between brands, check to see if the serving size is the same.

Calories count, so pay attention to the amount.

- This is where you'll find the number of calories per serving and the calories from fat in each serving.

- Fat-free doesn't mean calorie-free. Lower fat items may have as many calories as full-fat versions.

- If the label lists that 1 serving equals 3 cookies and 100 calories, and you eat 6 cookies, you've eaten 2 servings, or twice the number of calories and fat.

Look for foods that are rich in these nutrients.

- Use the label not only to limit fat and sodium, but also to increase nutrients that promote good health and may protect you from disease.

- Some Americans don't get enough vitamins A and C, potassium, calcium, and iron, so choose the brand with the higher % DV for these nutrients.

- Get the most nutrition for your calories—compare the calories to the nutrients you would be getting to make a healthier food choice.

Know your fats and reduce sodium for your health.

- To help reduce your risk of heart disease, use the label to select foods that are lowest in saturated fat, trans fat and cholesterol.

- Trans fat doesn't have a % DV, but consume as little as possible because it increases your risk of heart disease.

- The % DV for total fat includes all different kinds of fats.

- To help lower blood cholesterol, replace saturated and trans fats with monounsaturated and polyunsaturated fats found in fish, nuts, and liquid vegetable oils.

- Limit sodium to help reduce your risk of high blood pressure.

Reach for healthy, wholesome carbohydrates.

- Fiber and sugars are types of carbohydrates. Healthy sources, like fruits, vegetables, beans, and whole grains, can reduce the risk of heart disease and improve digestive functioning.

- Whole grain foods can't always be identified by color or name, such as multi-grain or wheat. Look for the "whole" grain listed first in the ingredient list, such as whole wheat, brown rice, or whole oats.

- There isn't a % DV for sugar, but you can compare the sugar content in grams among products.

- Limit foods with added sugars (sucrose, glucose, fructose, corn or maple syrup), which add calories but not other nutrients, such as vitamins and minerals. Make sure that added sugars are not one of the first few items in the ingredients list.

For protein, choose foods that are lower in fat.

- Most Americans get plenty of protein, but not always from the healthiest sources.

- When choosing a food for its protein content, such as meat, poultry, dry beans, milk and milk products, make choices that are lean, low-fat, or fat free.

The % Daily Value is a key to a balanced diet.

The % DV is a general guide to help you link nutrients in a serving of food to their contribution to your total daily diet. It can help you determine if a food is high or low in a nutrient—5% or less is low, 20% or more is high. You can use the % DV to make dietary trade-offs with other foods throughout the day. The * is a reminder that the % DV is based on a 2,000-calorie diet. You may need more or less, but the % DV is still a helpful gauge.

Nutrition Facts

Serving Size 1 cup (228g)
Servings Per Container 2

Amount Per Serving

Calories 250	Calories from Fat 110

	% Daily Value*
Total Fat 12g	18%
Saturated Fat 3g	15%
Trans Fat 3g	
Cholesterol 30mg	10%
Sodium 470mg	20%
Potassium 700mg	20%
Total Carbohydrate 31g	10%
Dietary Fiber 0g	0%
Sugars 5g	
Protein 5g	
Vitamin A	4%
Vitamin C	2%
Calcium	20%
Iron	4%

* Percent Daily Values are based on a 2,000 calorie diet. Your Daily Values may be higher or lower depending on your calorie needs.

		Calories:	2,000	2,500
Total fat	Less than		65g	80g
Sat fat	Less than		20g	25g
Cholesterol	Less than		300mg	300mg
Sodium	Less than		2,400mg	2,400mg
Total Carbohydrate			300g	375g
Dietary Fiber			25g	30g

U.S. Department of Health and Human Services, U.S. Department of Agriculture, For more information, visit www.healthierus.gov/dietaryguidelines

Appendix A2

DIETARY GUIDELINES FOR AMERICANS 2005
www.healthierus.gov/dietaryguidelines

Working Together...*Dietary Guidelines,* Food Guidance System, Food Label

The ***Dietary Guidelines for Americans*** are the cornerstone of federal nutrition policy and education. They are based on what experts have determined to be the best scientific knowledge about diet, physical activity and other issues related to what we should eat and how much physical activity we need. The *Dietary Guidelines* answer the questions, "What should Americans eat, how should we prepare our food to keep it safe and wholesome, and how should we be active to be healthy?" The *Dietary Guidelines* are designed to help Americans choose diets that will meet nutrient requirements, promote health, support active lives and reduce risks of chronic disease.

The *Dietary Guidelines* are a foundation of the **Food Guidance System**, which presents the science in a consumer-friendly form that helps people to be healthier by applying the science to their own lives. The Food Guidance System updates the Food Guide Pyramid, which was released in 1992. This new educational tool incorporates the updated 2005 *Dietary Guidelines* and makes recommendations on what and how much to eat.

Nutrition labeling is required for most packaged foods. In the "Nutrition Facts" panel, manufacturers are required to provide information on certain nutrients. The required nutrients were selected because they address today's health concerns. The order in which they must appear reflects the priority of dietary recommendations. The serving size is the basis for the calorie and nutrient declarations on the label.   The percent Daily Value (% DV) provides consumers an easy way to interpret the quantitative amounts without doing math. Another part of the food label that is important for consumers to use the ingredient list. The ingredient list is required on all foods that have more than one ingredient. Each ingredient is listed in descending order of predominance.

The Nutrition Facts panel provides information on what is in foods and the number of servings in the package. The Nutrition Facts panel in combination with the ingredient list, the name of the food (e.g., "Whole Wheat Bread", and certain claims (e.g., "high fiber", "low fat) gives specificity so that discriminating choices can be made within and among food groups. Knowing how to interpret label facts enables consumers to accurately apply key *Dietary Guidelines* messages that correspond to the nutrients and other information listed on the Facts panel

How do these work together?

The *Dietary Guidelines* provides information for all Americans on what makes a healthy diet. The consumer brochure, *Finding Your Way to a Healthier You:* Based on the *Dietary Guidelines for Americans,* provides tested messages that motivate consumers to pursue a healthy lifestyle. The *Dietary Guidelines* provides the key recommendations that can help dietitians and their clients develop achievable, measurable goals. The Food Guidance system and food label are the tools that clients can use to meet their goals.

For example, the *Dietary Guidelines* recommends consuming 3 or more ounce-equivalents of whole grain products per day, with at least half of grains coming from whole grains. The Food Guidance System would help identify the total number of grains recommended at a client's individual calorie level. The food label, particularly the ingredient list, would help the client identify which products contain whole grains. The Nutrition Facts panel would give the consumer information to select products that are high in fiber and lower in sodium and saturated fat.

The Food Guidance System and the food label are tools that consumers can use to meet the recommendations in the *Dietary Guidelines*, and to assist dietitians in personalizing the recommendations for their clients' needs.

Dietary Guidelines for Americans 2005. www.healthierus.gov/dietaryguidelines

Appendix B1

Examples of FDA-Approved Nutrient Content Health Claims

Claim	Definition
Calorie Free	<5 kcal per reference amount and per labeled serving
Low Calorie	≤40 kcal per reference amount
Reduced/Less Calories	At least 25% fewer calories than an appropriate reference food
Fat Free	<0.5 g per reference amount and per labeled serving
Low Fat	≤3 g per reference amount
Reduced/Less Fat	At least 25% less fat than an appropriate reference food
Saturated Fat Free	<0.5 g and <0.5 g trans fat per reference amount and per labeled serving
Low Saturated Fat	≤1 g per reference amount and ≤15% calories from saturated fat
Reduced/ Less Saturated Fat	At least 25% less saturated fat than an appropriate reference food
Cholesterol Free	<2 mg per reference amount and per labeled serving
Low Cholesterol	≤20 mg per reference amount
Reduced Cholesterol	At least 25% less cholesterol than an appropriate reference food
Sodium Free	<5 mg per reference amount and per labeled serving
Low Sodium	≤140 mg per reference amount
Reduced/Less Sodium	At least 25% less sodium than an appropriate reference food
Sugar Free	<0.5 g per reference amount and per labeled serving
Reduced/Less Sugar	At least 25% less sugar than an appropriate reference food
Light or Lite	If the product has more than 50% fat, it must be reduced by at least 50% per reference amount. Other products: fat must be reduced by at least 50% or kilocalories reduced by at least 1/3 per reference amount
Healthy	A food that is low in fat and saturated fat, has no more than 60 mg cholesterol, 360-480 mg sodium, and has at least 10% of the Daily Value for vitamin A, vitamin C, protein, calcium, iron, or fiber
Good Source	A serving must contain 10-19% of the Daily Value for the nutrient claimed
High	A serving must contain at least 20% of the Daily Value for the nutrient claimed
Lean	<10 g fat, 4.5 g saturated fat, and 95 mg cholesterol per serving (or 100 g of a food)
Extra Lean	<5 g fat, 2 g saturated fat, and 95 mg cholesterol per serving (or 100 g of a food)

Table 1. Examples of FDA-Approved Nutrient Content Claims

Visit the FDA website (www.fda.gov) for more claims, updated information, and more details on synonyms for the descriptors, definitions, and comments.

Appendix B2

Examples of FDA-Approved Health Claims

Food, Food Component, or Dietary Supplement Ingredient	Disease or Health-Related Condition
Calcium	Osteoporosis
Sodium	Hypertension
Dietary fat	Cancer
Dietary saturated fat and cholesterol	Risk of coronary artery disease
Fiber-containing grain products, fruits, and vegetables	Cancer
Fruits, vegetables, and grain products that contain fiber, particularly soluble fiber	Risk of coronary heart disease (CHD)
Fruits and vegetables	Cancer
Folate	Neural tube defects
Dietary sugar alcohol	Dental caries
Soluble fiber from certain foods	Risk of CHD
Soy protein	Risk of CHD
Plant sterol/stanol esters	Risk of CHD
Whole-grain foods	Risk of heart disease and certain cancers
Potassium	Risk of high blood pressure and stroke

A qualified health claim explains the relationship between a substance and a disease or health-related condition. An FDA-approved health claim may be used on both conventional foods and dietary supplements, provided that the substance in the product and the product itself meet the appropriate standards. Health claims are designed to be used by the general population or designated subgroups (e.g., the elderly) and are intended to assist the consumer in making healthy food choices.

Visit the FDA website (www.fda.gov) for updated approved claims and additional information about food products, claim requirements, model claim statements, and general criteria all claims must meet.

Appendix C1

Vitamin and Mineral Table

Nutrient	Adult Dietary Reference Intakes (DRI) (19–50 years)*	Tolerable Upper Intake Level	Basic Function	Common Sources
Vitamins				
B1 (Thiamin)	1.2 mg (females) 1.2 mg (males)	Not Determinable	Energy metabolism, nervous system	Whole grains, fortified grains, pork, beans/legumes, seeds
B2 (Riboflavin)	1.1 mg (females) 1.3 mg (males)	Not Determinable	Energy metabolism, skin development	Whole and fortified grains, milk, green leafy vegetables, meats
B3 (Niacin)	14 mg (females) 16 mg (males)	35 mg	Energy metabolism, component of nicotinamide adenine dinucleotide (NAD)	Whole grains, processed grains, animal products, nuts
B6 (Pyridoxine)	1.3 mg 1.5 mg (females 50+) 1.7 mg (males 50+)	100 mg	Glycogenolysis, gluconeogenesis, red blood cell formation, hemoglobin synthesis, nonessential amino acid synthesis, homocysteine metabolism	Whole grains, green leafy vegetables, beans, bananas, meat, fish, poultry
B12 (Cobalamin)	2.4 µg	Not Determinable	Cell synthesis, nervous system, red blood cells, homocysteine metabolism, activation of folate	Animal foods and fortified foods
Folate	400 µg	1,000 µg	Cell synthesis, red blood cell formation, homocysteine metabolism, neural tube development	Whole grains, fortified grains, beans, green leafy vegetables, orange juice
Pantothenic Acid	5 mg	Not Determinable	Energy metabolism	Many foods

*Unless noted

Nutrient	Adult Dietary Reference Intakes (DRI) (19-50 years)*	Tolerable Upper Intake Level	Basic Function	Common Sources
Vitamins				
Biotin	30 µg	Not Determinable	Energy metabolism	Many foods
Vitamin C	75 mg (females) 90 mg (females)	2,000 mg	Antioxidant, collagen synthesis, immune function, nonheme iron absorption	Citrus fruits, strawberries, broccoli, peppers, cabbage, tomatoes
Vitamin A	700 µg (females) 900 µg (males)	3,000 µg	Antioxidant, cell membrane health, vision	Retinoid form: animal foods, liver, fortified milk. Carotenoid form: orange, red, and yellow fruits and vegetables, green leafy vegetables
Vitamin D	5 µg 10 µg (ages 51-70) 15 µg (age 71+)	50 µg	Calcium and phosphorus balance, bone mineralization	Synthesized from sunlight, milk, fish oils, fortified foods
Vitamin E	15 mg	1,000 mg	Antioxidant	Whole grains, nuts, seeds, vegetable oils (much is lost with deep frying)
Vitamin K	90 µg	Not Determinable	Blood clotting	Produced by gut, liver, green leafy vegetables
Minerals				
Calcium	1,000 mg (ages 19-50) 1,200 mg (ages 51+)	2,500 mg	Bone mineralization, muscle contraction, nerve conduction	Dairy products, green leafy vegetables, fish with bones, fortified products
Iron	8 mg males 18 mg (females) 8 mg (females age 51+)	45 mg	Component of hemoglobin, immune system	Heme (well-absorbed) sources: red meat, other meat, fish, poultry. Nonheme (lesser absorbed) sources: beans/legumes, green leafy vegetables, dried fruit, fortified grains
Magnesium	310 mg (females 19-30) 320 mg (females 31+) 400 mg (males 19-30)	350 mg in supplemental form	Bone formation, coenzyme	Green leafy vegetables, nuts, seeds, beans/legumes

*Unless noted

Nutrient	Adult Dietary Reference Intakes (DRI) (19-50 years)*	Tolerable Upper Intake Level	Basic Function	Common Sources
Minerals				
Zinc	8 mg (females) 11 mg (males)	40 mg	Antioxidant coenzyme, immune system	Whole grains, animal foods
Boron	Not Established	20 mg	Calcium metabolism	Green leafy vegetables, some fruit
Chromium	25 µg (females 19-50) 20 µg (females 51+) 35 µg (males 19-50) 30 µg (males 51+)	Not determinable, but use caution with more than 200 µg	Energy metabolism, insulin action	Whole grains, mushrooms, beer
Copper	900 µg	10,000 µg	Antioxidant coenzyme, hemoglobin synthesis	Whole grains, seafood, nuts, seeds, beans
Fluoride	3 mg (females) 4 mg (males)	10 mg	Component in bones and teeth	Fluoridated water (usually from a municipal source), supplements
Iodine	150 µg	1,100 µg	Thyroid hormones	Salt-water fish, mushrooms, eggs, iodized salt
Manganese	1.8 mg (females) 2.3 mg (males)	11 mg	Bone formation, energy metabolism	Whole grains, beans, nuts
Molybdenum	45 µg	2,000 µg	Coenzyme	Whole grains, nuts, legumes
Phosphorus	700 mg	4,000 mg (19-70) 3,000 mg (71+)	Bone, phospholipids in cell membranes, adenosine triphosphate (ATP), cellular metabolism	Animal foods, many other foods
Selenium	55 µg	400 µg	Antioxidant enzymes	Many foods (dependent on soil content)

*Unless noted

Appendix C2

Dietary Reference Intakes (DRIs)

Dietary Reference Intakes (DRIs): Recommended Intakes for Individuals, Vitamins
Food and Nutrition Board, Institute of Medicine, National Academies

Life Stage Group	Vit A (µg/d)[a]	Vit C (mg/d)	Vit D (µg/d)[b,c]	Vit E (mg/d)[d]	Vit K (µg/d)	Thiamin (mg/d)	Riboflavin (mg/d)	Niacin (mg/d)[e]	Vit B6 (mg/d)	Folate (µg/d)[f]	Vit B12 (µg/d)	Pantothenic Acid (mg/d)	Biotin (µg/d)	Choline (mg/d)[g]
Infants														
0–6 mo	400*	40*	5*	4*	2.0*	0.2*	0.3*	2*	0.1*	65*	0.4*	1.7*	5*	125*
7–12 mo	500*	50*	5*	5*	2.5*	0.3*	0.4*	4*	0.3*	80*	0.5*	1.8*	6*	150*
Children														
1–3 y	300	15	5*	6	30*	0.5	0.5	6	0.5	150	0.9	2*	8*	200*
4–8 y	400	25	5*	7	55*	0.6	0.6	8	0.6	200	1.2	3*	12*	250*
Males														
9–13 y	600	45	5*	11	60*	0.9	0.9	12	1.0	300	1.8	4*	20*	375*
14–18 y	900	75	5*	15	75*	1.2	1.3	16	1.3	400	2.4	5*	25*	550*
19–30 y	900	90	5*	15	120*	1.2	1.3	16	1.3	400	2.4	5*	30*	550*
31–50 y	900	90	5*	15	120*	1.2	1.3	16	1.3	400	2.4	5*	30*	550*
51–70 y	900	90	10*	15	120*	1.2	1.3	16	1.7	400	2.4[i]	5*	30*	550*
>70 y	900	90	15*	15	120*	1.2	1.3	16	1.7	400	2.4[i]	5*	30*	550*
Females														
9–13 y	600	45	5*	11	60*	0.9	0.9	12	1.0	300	1.8	4*	20*	375*
14–18 y	700	65	5*	15	75*	1.0	1.0	14	1.2	400[i]	2.4	5*	25*	400*
19–30 y	700	75	5*	15	90*	1.1	1.1	14	1.3	400[i]	2.4	5*	30*	425*
31–50 y	700	75	5*	15	90*	1.1	1.1	14	1.3	400[i]	2.4	5*	30*	425*
51–70 y	700	75	10*	15	90*	1.1	1.1	14	1.5	400	2.4[h]	5*	30*	425*
>70 y	700	75	15*	15	90*	1.1	1.1	14	1.5	400	2.4[h]	5*	30*	425*
Pregnancy														
14–18 y	750	80	5*	15	75*	1.4	1.4	18	1.9	600[j]	2.6	6*	30*	450*
19–30 y	770	85	5*	15	90*	1.4	1.4	18	1.9	600[j]	2.6	6*	30*	450*
31–50 y	770	85	5*	15	90*	1.4	1.4	18	1.9	600[j]	2.6	6*	30*	450*
Lactation														
14–18 y	1,200	115	5*	19	75*	1.4	1.6	17	2.0	500	2.8	7*	35*	550*
19–30 y	1,300	120	5*	19	90*	1.4	1.6	17	2.0	500	2.8	7*	35*	550*
31–50 y	1,300	120	5*	19	90*	1.4	1.6	17	2.0	500	2.8	7*	35*	550*

NOTE: This table (taken from the DRI reports, see www.nap.edu) presents Recommended Dietary Allowances (RDAs) in **bold type** and Adequate Intakes (AIs) in ordinary type followed by an asterisk (*). RDAs and AIs may both be used as goals for individual intake. RDAs are set to meet the needs of almost all (97 to 98 percent) individuals in a group. For healthy breastfed infants, the AI is the mean intake. The AI for other life stage and gender groups is believed to cover needs of all individuals in the group, but lack of data or uncertainty in the data prevent being able to specify with confidence the percentage of individuals covered by this intake.

[a] As retinol activity equivalents (RAEs). 1 RAE = 1 µg retinol, 12 µg β-carotene, 24 µg α-carotene, or 24 µg β-cryptoxanthin. The RAE for dietary provitamin A carotenoids is twofold greater than retinol equivalents (RE), whereas the RAE for preformed vitamin A is the same as RE.

[b] As cholecalciferol. 1 µg cholecalciferol = 40 IU vitamin D.

[c] In the absence of adequate exposure to sunlight.

[d] As α-tocopherol. α-Tocopherol includes *RRR*-α-tocopherol, the only form of α-tocopherol that occurs naturally in foods, and the 2*R*-stereoisomeric forms of α-tocopherol (*RRR*-, *RSR*-, *RRS*-, and *RSS*-α-tocopherol) that occur in fortified foods and supplements. It does not include the 2*S*-stereoisomeric forms of α-tocopherol (*SRR*-, *SSR*-, *SRS*-, and *SSS*-α-tocopherol), also found in fortified foods and supplements.

[e] As niacin equivalents (NE). 1 mg of niacin = 60 mg of tryptophan 0–6 months = preformed niacin (not NE).

[f] As dietary folate equivalents (DFE). 1 DFE = 1 µg food folate = 0.6 µg folic acid from fortified food or as a supplement consumed with food = 0.5 µg of a supplement taken on an empty stomach.

[g] Although AIs have been set for choline, there are few data to assess whether a dietary supply of choline is needed at all stages of the life cycle, and it may be that the choline requirement can be met by endogenous synthesis at some of these stages.

[h] Because 10 to 30 percent of older people may malabsorb food-bound B₁₂, it is advisable for those older than 50 years to meet their RDA mainly by consuming foods fortified with B₁₂ or a supplement containing B₁₂.

[i] In view of evidence linking folate intake with neural tube defects in the fetus, it is recommended that all women capable of becoming pregnant consume 400 µg from supplements or fortified foods in addition to intake of food folate from a varied diet.

[j] It is assumed that women will continue consuming 400 µg from supplements or fortified food until their pregnancy is confirmed and they enter prenatal care, which ordinarily occurs after the end of the periconceptional period—the critical time for formation of the neural tube.

Dietary Reference Intakes (DRIs): Recommended Intakes for Individuals, Elements
Food and Nutrition Board, Institute of Medicine, National Academies

Life Stage Group	Calcium (mg/d)	Chromium (µg/d)	Copper (µg/d)	Fluoride (mg/d)	Iodine (µg/d)	Iron (mg/d)	Magnesium (mgd)	Manganese (mg/d)	Molybdenum (µg/d)	Phosphorus (mg/d)	Selenium (µg/d)	Zinc (mg/d)	Potassium (g/d)	Sodium (g/d)	Chloride (g/d)
Infants															
0–6 mo	210*	0.2*	200*	0.01*	110*	0.27*	30*	0.003*	2*	100*	15*	2*	0.4*	0.12*	0.18*
7–12 mo	270*	5.5*	220*	0.5*	130*	11	75*	0.6*	3*	275*	20*	3	0.7*	0.37*	0.57*
Children															
1–3 y	500*	11*	340	0.7*	90	7	80	1.2*	17	460	20	3	3.0*	1.0*	1.5*
4–8 y	800*	15*	440	1*	90	10	130	1.5*	22	500	30	5	3.8*	1.2*	1.9*
Males															
9–13 y	1,300*	25*	700	2*	120	8	240	1.9*	34	1,250	40	8	4.5*	1.5*	2.3*
14–18 y	1,300*	35*	890	3*	150	11	410	2.2*	43	1,250	55	11	4.7*	1.5*	2.3*
19–30 y	1,000*	35*	900	4*	150	8	400	2.3*	45	700	55	11	4.7*	1.5*	2.3*
31–50 y	1,000*	35*	900	4*	150	8	420	2.3*	45	700	55	11	4.7*	1.5*	2.3*
51–70 y	1,200*	30*	900	4*	150	8	420	2.3*	45	700	55	11	4.7*	1.3*	2.0*
>70 y	1,200*	30*	900	4*	150	8	420	2.3*	45	700	55	11	4.7*	1.2*	1.8*
Females															
9–13 y	1,300*	21*	700	2*	120	8	240	1.6*	34	1,250	40	8	4.5*	1.5*	2.3*
14–18 y	1,300*	24*	890	3*	150	15	360	1.6*	43	1,250	55	9	4.7*	1.5*	2.3*
19–30 y	1,000*	25*	900	3*	150	18	310	1.8*	45	700	55	8	4.7*	1.5*	2.3*
31–50 y	1,000*	25*	900	3*	150	18	320	1.8*	45	700	55	8	4.7*	1.5*	2.3*
51–70 y	1,200*	20*	900	3*	150	8	320	1.8*	45	700	55	8	4.7*	1.3*	2.0*
>70 y	1,200*	20*	900	3*	150	8	320	1.8*	45	700	55	8	4.7*	1.2*	1.8*
Pregnancy															
14–18 y	1,300*	29*	1,000	3*	220	27	400	2.0*	50	1,250	60	12	4.7*	1.5*	2.3*
19–30 y	1,000*	30*	1,000	3*	220	27	350	2.0*	50	700	60	11	4.7*	1.5*	2.3*
31–50 y	1,000*	30*	1,000	3*	220	27	360	2.0*	50	700	60	11	4.7*	1.5*	2.3*
Lactation															
14–18 y	1,300*	44*	1,300	3*	290	10	360	2.6*	50	1,250	70	13	5.1*	1.5*	2.3*
19–30 y	1,000*	45*	1,300	3*	290	9	310	2.6*	50	700	70	12	5.1*	1.5*	2.3*
31–50 y	1,000*	45*	1,300	3*	290	9	320	2.6*	50	700	70	12	5.1*	1.5*	2.3*

NOTE: This table presents Recommended Dietary Allowances (RDAs) in **bold type** and Adequate Intakes (AIs) in ordinary type followed by an asterisk (*). RDAs and AIs may both be used as goals for individual intake. RDAs are set to meet the needs of almost all (97 to 98 percent) individuals in a group. For healthy breastfed infants, the AI is the mean intake. The AI for other life stage and gender groups is believed to cover needs of all individuals in the group, but lack of data or uncertainty in the data prevent being able to specify with confidence the percentage of individuals covered by this intake.

SOURCES: *Dietary Reference Intakes for Calcium, Phosphorous, Magnesium, Vitamin D, and Fluoride (1997); Dietary Reference Intakes for Thiamin, Riboflavin, Niacin, Vitamin B₆, Folate, Vitamin B₁₂, Pantothenic Acid, Biotin, and Choline (1998); Dietary Reference Intakes for Vitamin C, Vitamin E, Selenium, and Carotenoids (2000); Dietary Reference Intakes for Vitamin A, Vitamin K, Arsenic, Boron, Chromium, Copper, Iodine, Iron, Manganese, Molybdenum, Nickel, Silicon, Vanadium, and Zinc (2001); and Dietary Reference Intakes for Water, Potassium, Sodium, Chloride, and Sulfate (2004).* These reports may be accessed via http://www.nap.edu.

Dietary Reference Intakes (DRIs): Tolerable Upper Intake Levels (UL[a]), Vitamins
Food and Nutrition Board, Institute of Medicine, National Academies

Life Stage Group	Vitamin A (µg/d)[b]	Vitamin C (mg/d)	Vitamin D (µg/d)	Vitamin E (mg/d)[c,d]	Vitamin K	Thiamin	Riboflavin	Niacin (mg/d)[d]	Vitamin B6 (mg/d)	Folate (µg/d)[d]	Vitamin B12	Pantothenic Acid	Biotin	Choline (g/d)	Carotenoids[e]
Infants															
0–6 mo	600	ND[f]	25	ND	ND	ND	ND	ND	ND	ND	ND	ND	ND	ND	ND
7–12 mo	600	ND	25	ND	ND	ND	ND	ND	ND	ND	ND	ND	ND	ND	ND
Children															
1–3 y	600	400	50	200	ND	ND	ND	10	30	300	ND	ND	ND	1.0	ND
4–8 y	900	650	50	300	ND	ND	ND	15	40	400	ND	ND	ND	1.0	ND
Males, Females															
9–13 y	1,700	1,200	50	600	ND	ND	ND	20	60	600	ND	ND	ND	2.0	ND
14–18 y	2,800	1,800	50	800	ND	ND	ND	30	80	800	ND	ND	ND	3.0	ND
19–70 y	3,000	2,000	50	1,000	ND	ND	ND	35	100	1,000	ND	ND	ND	3.5	ND
>70 y	3,000	2,000	50	1,000	ND	ND	ND	35	100	1,000	ND	ND	ND	3.5	ND
Pregnancy															
14–18 y	2,800	1,800	50	800	ND	ND	ND	30	80	800	ND	ND	ND	3.0	ND
19–50 y	3,000	2,000	50	1,000	ND	ND	ND	35	100	1,000	ND	ND	ND	3.5	ND
Lactation															
14–18 y	2,800	1,800	50	800	ND	ND	ND	30	80	800	ND	ND	ND	3.0	ND
19–50 y	3,000	2,000	50	1,000	ND	ND	ND	35	100	1,000	ND	ND	ND	3.5	ND

[a] UL = The maximum level of daily nutrient intake that is likely to pose no risk of adverse effects. Unless otherwise specified, the UL represents total intake from food, water, and supplements. Due to lack of suitable data, ULs could not be established for vitamin K, thiamin, riboflavin, vitamin B12, pantothenic acid, biotin, carotenoids. In the absence of ULs, extra caution may be warranted in consuming levels above recommended intakes.

[b] As preformed vitamin A only.

[c] As α-tocopherol; applies to any form of supplemental α-tocopherol.

[d] The ULs for vitamin E, niacin, and folate apply to synthetic forms obtained from supplements, fortified foods, or a combination of the two.

[e] β-Carotene supplements are advised only to serve as a provitamin A source for individuals at risk of vitamin A deficiency.

[f] ND = Not determinable due to lack of data of adverse effects in this age group and concern with regard to lack of ability to handle excess amounts. Source of intake should be from food only to prevent high levels of intake.

SOURCES: *Dietary Reference Intakes for Calcium, Phosphorous, Magnesium, Vitamin D, and Fluoride* (1997); *Dietary Reference Intakes for Thiamin, Riboflavin, Niacin, Vitamin B6, Folate, Vitamin B12, Pantothenic Acid, Biotin, and Choline* (1998); *Dietary Reference Intakes for Vitamin C, Vitamin E, Selenium, and Carotenoids* (2000); and *Dietary Reference Intakes for Vitamin A, Vitamin K, Arsenic, Boron, Chromium, Copper, Iodine, Iron, Manganese, Molybdenum, Nickel, Silicon, Vanadium, and Zinc* (2001). These reports may be accessed via http://www.nap.edu.

Dietary Reference Intakes (DRIs): Tolerable Upper Intake Levels (UL[a]), Elements
Food and Nutrition Board, Institute of Medicine, National Academies

Life Stage Group	Arsenic[b]	Boron (mg/d)	Calcium (g/d)	Chromium	Copper (μg/d)	Fluoride (mg/d)	Iodine (μg/d)	Iron (mg/d)	Magnesium (mg/d)[c]	Manganese (mg/d)	Molybdenum (μg/d)	Nickel (mg/d)	Phosphorus (g/d)	Potassium	Selenium (μg/d)	Silicon[d]	Sulfate	Vanadium (mg/d)[e]	Zinc (mg/d)	Sodium (g/d)	Chloride (g/d)
Infants																					
0–6 mo	ND[f]	ND	ND	ND	ND	0.7	ND	40	ND	ND	ND	ND	ND	ND	45	ND	ND	ND	4	ND	ND
7–12 mo	ND	ND	ND	ND	ND	0.9	ND	40	ND	ND	ND	ND	ND	ND	60	ND	ND	ND	5	ND	ND
Children																					
1–3 y	ND	3	2.5	ND	1,000	1.3	200	40	65	2	300	0.2	3	ND	90	ND	ND	ND	7	1.5	2.3
4–8 y	ND	6	2.5	ND	3,000	2.2	300	40	110	3	600	0.3	3	ND	150	ND	ND	ND	12	1.9	2.9
Males, Females																					
9–13 y	ND	11	2.5	ND	5,000	10	600	40	350	6	1,100	0.6	4	ND	280	ND	ND	ND	23	2.2	3.4
14–18 y	ND	17	2.5	ND	8,000	10	900	45	350	9	1,700	1.0	4	ND	400	ND	ND	ND	34	2.3	3.6
19–70 y	ND	20	2.5	ND	10,000	10	1,100	45	350	11	2,000	1.0	4	ND	400	ND	ND	1.8	40	2.3	3.6
>70 y	ND	20	2.5	ND	10,000	10	1,100	45	350	11	2,000	1.0	3	ND	400	ND	ND	1.8	40	2.3	3.6
Pregnancy																					
14–18 y	ND	17	2.5	ND	8,000	10	900	45	350	9	1,700	1.0	3.5	ND	400	ND	ND	ND	34	2.3	3.6
19–50 y	ND	20	2.5	ND	10,000	10	1,100	45	350	11	2,000	1.0	3.5	ND	400	ND	ND	ND	40	2.3	3.6
Lactation																					
14–18 y	ND	17	2.5	ND	8,000	10	900	45	350	9	1,700	1.0	4	ND	400	ND	ND	ND	34	2.3	3.6
19–50 y	ND	20	2.5	ND	10,000	10	1,100	45	350	11	2,000	1.0	4	ND	400	ND	ND	ND	40	2.3	3.6

[a] UL = The maximum level of daily nutrient intake that is likely to pose no risk of adverse effects. Unless otherwise specified, the UL represents total intake from food, water, and supplements. Due to lack of suitable data, ULs could not be established for arsenic, chromium, silicon, potassium, and sulfate. In the absence of ULs, extra caution may be warranted in consuming levels above recommended intakes.

[b] Although the UL was not determined for arsenic, there is no justification for adding arsenic to food or supplements.

[c] The ULs for magnesium represent intake from a pharmacological agent only and do not include intake from food and water.

[d] Although silicon has not been shown to cause adverse effects in humans, there is no justification for adding silicon to supplements.

[e] Although vanadium in food has not been shown to cause adverse effects in humans, there is no justification for adding vanadium to food and vanadium supplements should be used with caution. The UL is based on adverse effects in laboratory animals and this data could be used to set a UL for adults but not children and adolescents.

[f] ND = Not determinable due to lack of data of adverse effects in this age group and concern with regard to lack of ability to handle excess amounts. Source of intake should be from food only to prevent high levels of intake.

SOURCES: *Dietary Reference Intakes for Calcium, Phosphorous, Magnesium, Vitamin D, and Fluoride* (1997); *Dietary Reference Intakes for Thiamin, Riboflavin, Niacin, Vitamin B₆, Folate, Vitamin B₁₂, Pantothenic Acid, Biotin, and Choline* (1998); *Dietary Reference Intakes for Vitamin C, Vitamin E, Selenium, and Carotenoids* (2000); *Dietary Reference Intakes for Vitamin A, Vitamin K, Arsenic, Boron, Chromium, Copper, Iodine, Iron, Manganese, Molybdenum, Nickel, Silicon, Vanadium, and Zinc* (2001); and *Dietary Reference Intakes for Water, Potassium, Sodium, Chloride, and Sulfate* (2004). These reports may be accessed via http://www.nap.edu.

Dietary Reference Intakes (DRIs): Estimated Energy Requirements (EER) for Men and Women 30 Years of Age[a]

Food and Nutrition Board, Institute of Medicine, National Academies

Height (m [in])	PAL[b]	Weight for BMI[c] of 18.5 kg/m² (kg [lb])	Weight for BMI of 24.99 kg/m² (kg [lb])	EER, Men[d] (kcal/day)		EER, Women[d] (kcal/day)	
				BMI of 18.5 kg/m²	BMI of 24.99 kg/m²	BMI of 18.5 kg/m²	BMI of 24.99 kg/m²
1.50 (59)	Sedentary	41.6 (92)	56.2 (124)	1,848	2,080	1,625	1,762
	Low active			2,009	2,267	1,803	1,956
	Active			2,215	2,506	2,025	2,198
	Very active			2,554	2,898	2,291	2,489
1.65 (65)	Sedentary	50.4 (111)	68.0 (150)	2,068	2,349	1,816	1,982
	Low active			2,254	2,566	2,016	2,202
	Active			2,490	2,842	2,267	2,477
	Very active			2,880	3,296	2,567	2,807
1.80 (71)	Sedentary	59.9 (132)	81.0 (178)	2,301	2,635	2,015	2,211
	Low active			2,513	2,884	2,239	2,459
	Active			2,782	3,200	2,519	2,769
	Very active			3,225	3,720	2,855	3,141

[a] For each year below 30, add 7 kcal/day for women and 10 kcal/day for men. For each year above 30, subtract 7 kcal/day for women and 10 kcal/day for men.

[b] PAL = physical activity level.

[c] BMI = body mass index.

[d] Derived from the following regression equations based on doubly labeled water data:

Adult man: $EER = 662 - 9.53 \times age\ (y) + PA \times (15.91 \times wt\ [kg] + 539.6 \times ht\ [m])$

Adult woman: $EER = 354 - 6.91 \times age\ (y) + PA \times (9.36 \times wt\ [kg] + 726 \times ht\ [m])$

Where PA refers to coefficient for PAL

PAL = total energy expenditure ÷ basal energy expenditure

PA = 1.0 if PAL ≥ 1.0 < 1.4 (sedentary)

PA = 1.12 if PAL ≥ 1.4 < 1.6 (low active)

PA = 1.27 if PAL ≥ 1.6 < 1.9 (active)

PA = 1.45 if PAL ≥ 1.9 < 2.5 (very active)

Dietary Reference Intakes (DRIs): Acceptable Macronutrient Distribution Ranges

Food and Nutrition Board, Institute of Medicine, National Academies

Macronutrient	Range (percent of energy)		
	Children, 1–3 y	Children, 4–18 y	Adults
Fat	30–40	25–35	20–35
n-6 polyunsaturated fatty acids[a] (linoleic acid)	5–10	5–10	5–10
n-3 polyunsaturated fatty acids[a] (α-linolenic acid)	0.6–1.2	0.6–1.2	0.6–1.2
Carbohydrate	45–65	45–65	45–65
Protein	5–20	10–30	10–35

[a] Approximately 10% of the total can come from longer-chain n-3 or n-6 fatty acids.

SOURCE: *Dietary Reference Intakes for Energy, Carbohydrate, Fiber, Fat, Fatty Acids, Cholesterol, Protein, and Amino Acids* (2002).

Dietary Reference Intakes (DRIs): Recommended Intakes for Individuals, Macronutrients
Food and Nutrition Board, Institute of Medicine, National Academies

Life Stage Group	Total Water[a] (L/d)	Carbohydrate (g/d)	Total Fiber (g/d)	Fat (g/d)	Linoleic Acid (g/d)	α-Linolenic Acid (g/d)	Protein[b] (g/d)
Infants							
0–6 mo	0.7*	60*	ND	31*	4.4*	0.5*	9.1*
7–12 mo	0.8*	95*	ND	30*	4.6*	0.5*	**11.0**[c]
Children							
1–3 y	1.3*	**130**	19*	ND	7*	0.7*	**13**
4–8 y	1.7*	**130**	25*	ND	10*	0.9*	**19**
Males							
9–13 y	2.4*	**130**	31*	ND	12*	1.2*	**34**
14–18 y	3.3*	**130**	38*	ND	16*	1.6*	**52**
19–30 y	3.7*	**130**	38*	ND	17*	1.6*	**56**
31–50 y	3.7*	**130**	38*	ND	17*	1.6*	**56**
51–70 y	3.7*	**130**	30*	ND	14*	1.6*	**56**
> 70 y	3.7*	**130**	30*	ND	14*	1.6*	**56**
Females							
9–13 y	2.1*	**130**	26*	ND	10*	1.0*	**34**
14–18 y	2.3*	**130**	26*	ND	11*	1.1*	**46**
19–30 y	2.7*	**130**	25*	ND	12*	1.1*	**46**
31–50 y	2.7*	**130**	25*	ND	12*	1.1*	**46**
51–70 y	2.7*	**130**	21*	ND	11*	1.1*	**46**
> 70 y	2.7*	**130**	21*	ND	11*	1.1*	**46**
Pregnancy							
14–18 y	3.0*	**175**	28*	ND	13*	1.4*	**71**
19–30 y	3.0*	**175**	28*	ND	13*	1.4*	**71**
31–50 y	3.0*	**175**	28*	ND	13*	1.4*	**71**
Lactation							
14–18 y	3.8*	**210**	29*	ND	13*	1.3*	**71**
19–30 y	3.8*	**210**	29*	ND	13*	1.3*	**71**
31–50 y	3.8*	**210**	29*	ND	13*	1.3*	**71**

NOTE: This table presents Recommended Dietary Allowances (RDAs) in **bold** type and Adequate Intakes (AIs) in ordinary type followed by an asterisk (*). RDAs and AIs may both be used as goals for individual intake. RDAs are set to meet the needs of almost all (97 to 98 percent) individuals in a group. For healthy infants fed human milk, the AI is the mean intake. The AI for other life stage and gender groups is believed to cover the needs of all individuals in the group, but lack of data or uncertainty in the data prevent being able to specify with confidence the percentage of individuals covered by this intake.

[a] *Total* water includes all water contained in food, beverages, and drinking water.
[b] Based on 0.8 g/kg body weight for the reference body weight.
[c] Change from 13.5 in prepublication copy due to calculation error.

Dietary Reference Intakes (DRIs): Additional Macronutrient Recommendations
Food and Nutrition Board, Institute of Medicine, National Academies

Macronutrient	Recommendation
Dietary cholesterol	As low as possible while consuming a nutritionally adequate diet
Trans fatty acids	As low as possible while consuming a nutritionally adequate diet
Saturated fatty acids	As low as possible while consuming a nutritionally adequate diet
Added sugars	Limit to no more than 25% of total energy

SOURCE: *Dietary Reference Intakes for Energy, Carbohydrate, Fiber, Fat, Fatty Acids, Cholesterol, Protein, and Amino Acids (2002).*

Dietary Reference Intakes (DRIs): Estimated Average Requirements for Groups
Food and Nutrition Board, Institute of Medicine, National Academies

Life Stage Group	CHO (g/d)	Protein (g/d)[a]	Vit A (µg/d)[b]	Vit C (mg/d)	Vit E (mg/d)[c]	Thiamin (mg/d)	Riboflavin (mg/d)	Niacin (mg/d)[d]	Vit B6 (mg/d)	Folate (µg/d)[e]	Vit B12 (µg/d)	Copper (µg/d)	Iodine (µg/d)	Iron (mg/d)	Magnesium (mg/d)	Molybdenum (µg/d)	Phosphorus (mg/d)	Selenium (µg/d)	Zinc (mg/d)
Infants																			
7–12 mo		9*												6.9					2.5
Children																			
1–3 y	100	11	210	13	5	0.4	0.4	5	0.4	120	0.7	260	65	3.0	65	13	380	17	2.5
4–8 y	100	15	275	22	6	0.5	0.5	6	0.5	160	1.0	340	65	4.1	110	17	405	23	4.0
Males																			
9–13 y	100	27	445	39	9	0.7	0.8	9	0.8	250	1.5	540	73	5.9	200	26	1,055	35	7.0
14–18 y	100	44	630	63	12	1.0	1.1	12	1.1	330	2.0	685	95	7.7	340	33	1,055	45	8.5
19–30 y	100	46	625	75	12	1.0	1.1	12	1.1	320	2.0	700	95	6	330	34	580	45	9.4
31–50 y	100	46	625	75	12	1.0	1.1	12	1.1	320	2.0	700	95	6	350	34	580	45	9.4
51–70 y	100	46	625	75	12	1.0	1.1	12	1.4	320	2.0	700	95	6	350	34	580	45	9.4
>70 y	100	46	625	75	12	1.0	1.1	12	1.4	320	2.0	700	95	6	350	34	580	45	9.4
Females																			
9–13 y	100	28	420	39	9	0.7	0.8	9	0.8	250	1.5	540	73	5.7	200	26	1,055	35	7.0
14–18 y	100	38	485	56	12	0.9	0.9	11	1.0	330	2.0	685	95	7.9	300	33	1,055	45	7.3
19–30 y	100	38	500	60	12	0.9	0.9	11	1.1	320	2.0	700	95	8.1	255	34	580	45	6.8
31–50 y	100	38	500	60	12	0.9	0.9	11	1.1	320	2.0	700	95	8.1	265	34	580	45	6.8
51–70 y	100	38	500	60	12	0.9	0.9	11	1.3	320	2.0	700	95	5	265	34	580	45	6.8
>70 y	100	38	500	60	12	0.9	0.9	11	1.3	320	2.0	700	95	5	265	34	580	45	6.8
Pregnancy																			
14–18 y	135	50	530	66	12	1.2	1.2	14	1.6	520	2.2	785	160	23	335	40	1,055	49	10.5
19–30 y	135	50	550	70	12	1.2	1.2	14	1.6	520	2.2	800	160	22	290	40	580	49	9.5
31–50 y	135	50	550	70	12	1.2	1.2	14	1.6	520	2.2	800	160	22	300	40	580	49	9.5
Lactation																			
14–18 y	160	60	885	96	16	1.2	1.3	13	1.7	450	2.4	985	209	7	300	35	1,055	59	10.9
19–30 y	160	60	900	100	16	1.2	1.3	13	1.7	450	2.4	1,000	209	6.5	255	36	580	59	10.4
31–50 y	160	60	900	100	16	1.2	1.3	13	1.7	450	2.4	1,000	209	6.5	265	36	580	59	10.4

NOTE: This table presents Estimated Average Requirements (EARs) which serve two purposes: for assessing adequacy of population intakes, and as the basis for calculating Recommended Dietary Allowances (RDAs) for individuals for those nutrients. EARs have not been established for vitamin D, vitamin K, pantothenic acid, biotin, choline, calcium, chromium, fluoride, manganese, or other nutrients not yet evaluated via the DRI process.

[a] For individual at reference weight (Table 1-1). *indicates change from prepublication copy due to calculation error.

[b] As retinol activity equivalents (RAEs). 1 RAE = 1 µg retinol, 12 µg β-carotene, 24 µg α-carotene, or 24 µg β-cryptoxanthin. The RAE for dietary provitamin A carotenoids is two-fold greater than retinol equivalents (RE), whereas the RAE for preformed vitamin A is the same as RE.

[c] As α-tocopherol. α-Tocopherol includes RRR-α-tocopherol, the only form of α-tocopherol that occurs naturally in foods, and the 2R-stereoisomeric forms of α-tocopherol (RRR-, RSR-, RRS-, and RSS-α-tocopherol) that occur in fortified foods and supplements. It does not include the 2S-stereoisomeric forms of α-tocopherol (SRR-, SSR-, SRS-, and SSS-α-tocopherol), also found in fortified foods and supplements.

[d] As niacin equivalents (NE). 1 mg of niacin = 60 mg of tryptophan.

[e] As dietary folate equivalents (DFE). 1 DFE = 1 µg food folate = 0.6 µg of folic acid from fortified food or as a supplement consumed with food = 0.5 µg of a supplement taken on an empty stomach.

SOURCES: Dietary Reference Intakes for Calcium, Phosphorous, Magnesium, Vitamin D, and Fluoride (1997); Dietary Reference Intakes for Thiamin, Riboflavin, Niacin, Vitamin B6, Folate, Vitamin B12, Pantothenic Acid, Biotin, and Choline (1998); Dietary Reference Intakes for Vitamin C, Vitamin E, Selenium, and Carotenoids (2000); Dietary Reference Intakes for Vitamin A, Vitamin K, Arsenic, Boron, Chromium, Copper, Iodine, Iron, Manganese, Molybdenum, Nickel, Silicon, Vanadium, and Zinc (2001), and Dietary Reference Intakes for Energy, Carbohydrate, Fiber, Fat, Fatty Acids, Cholesterol, Protein, and Amino Acids (2002). These reports may be accessed via www.nap.edu.

Appendix D1

MyPyramid

Food Intake Patterns

The suggested amounts of food to consume from the basic food groups, subgroups, and oils to meet recommended nutrient intakes at 12 different calorie levels. Nutrient and energy contributions from each group are calculated according to the nutrient-dense forms of foods in each group (e.g., lean meats and fat-free milk). The table also shows the discretionary calorie allowance that can be accommodated within each calorie level, in addition to the suggested amounts of nutrient-dense forms of foods in each group.

Daily Amount of Food From Each Group

Calorie Level[1]	1,000	1,200	1,400	1,600	1,800	2,000	2,200	2,400	2,600	2,800	3,000	3,200
Fruits[2]	1 cup	1 cup	1.5 cups	1.5 cups	1.5 cups	2 cups	2 cups	2 cups	2 cups	2.5 cups	2.5 cups	2.5 cups
Vegetables[3]	1 cup	1.5 cups	1.5 cups	2 cups	2.5 cups	2.5 cups	3 cups	3 cups	3.5 cups	3.5 cups	4 cups	4 cups
Grains[4]	3 oz-eq	4 oz-eq	5 oz-eq	5 oz-eq	6 oz-eq	6 oz-eq	7 oz-eq	8 oz-eq	9 oz-eq	10 oz-eq	10 oz-eq	10 oz-eq
Meat and Beans[5]	2 oz-eq	3 oz-eq	4 oz-eq	5 oz-eq	5 oz-eq	5.5 oz-eq	6 oz-eq	6.5 oz-eq	6.5 oz-eq	7 oz-eq	7 oz-eq	7 oz-eq
Milk[6]	2 cups	2 cups	2 cups	3 cups	3 cups	3 cups	3 cups	3 cups	3 cups	3 cups	3 cups	3 cups
Oils[7]	3 tsp	4 tsp	4 tsp	5 tsp	5 tsp	6 tsp	6 tsp	7 tsp	8 tsp	8 tsp	10 tsp	11 tsp
Discretionary calorie allowance[8]	165	171	171	132	195	267	290	362	410	426	512	648

1 **Calorie Levels** are set across a wide range to accommodate the needs of different individuals. The attached table "Estimated Daily Calorie Needs" can be used to help assign individuals to the food intake pattern at a particular calorie level.

2 **Fruit Group** includes all fresh, frozen, canned, and dried fruits and fruit juices. In general, 1 cup of fruit or 100% fruit juice, or 1/2 cup of dried fruit can be considered as 1 cup from the fruit group.

3 **Vegetable Group** includes all fresh, frozen, canned, and dried vegetables and vegetable juices. In general, 1 cup of raw or cooked vegetables or vegetable juice, or 2 cups of raw leafy greens can be considered as 1 cup from the vegetable group.

Vegetable Subgroup Amounts are Per Week

Calorie Level	1,000	1,200	1,400	1,600	1,800	2,000	2,200	2,400	2,600	2,800	3,000	3,200
Dark green veg.	1 c/wk	1.5 c/wk	1.5 c/wk	2 c/wk	3 c/wk	3 c/wk	3 c/wk	3 c/wk	3 c/wk	3 c/wk	3 c/wk	3 c/wk
Orange veg.	.5 c/wk	1 c/wk	1 c/wk	1.5 c/wk	2 c/wk	2 c/wk	2 c/wk	2 c/wk	2.5 c/wk	2.5 c/wk	2.5 c/wk	2.5 c/wk
Legumes	.5 c/wk	1 c/wk	1 c/wk	2.5 c/wk	3 c/wk	3 c/wk	3 c/wk	3 c/wk	3.5 c/wk	3.5 c/wk	3.5 c/wk	3.5 c/wk
Starchy veg.	1.5 c/wk	2.5 c/wk	2.5 c/wk	2.5 c/wk	3 c/wk	3 c/wk	6 c/wk	6 c/wk	7 c/wk	7 c/wk	9 c/wk	9 c/wk
Other veg.	3.5 c/wk	4.5 c/wk	4.5 c/wk	5.5 c/wk	6.5 c/wk	6.5 c/wk	7 c/wk	7 c/wk	8.5 c/wk	8.5 c/wk	10 c/wk	10 c/wk

4 **Grains Group** includes all foods made from wheat, rice, oats, cornmeal, barley, such as bread, pasta, oatmeal, breakfast cereals, tortillas, and grits. In general, 1 slice of bread, 1 cup of ready-to-eat cereal, or 1/2 cup of cooked rice, pasta, or cooked cereal can be considered as 1 ounce equivalent from the grains group. **At least half of all grains consumed should be whole grains.**

5 **Meat & Beans Group** in general, 1 ounce of lean meat, poultry, or fish, 1 egg, 1 Tbsp. peanut butter, 1/4 cup cooked dry beans, or 1/2 ounce of nuts or seeds can be considered as 1 ounce equivalent from the meat and beans group.

6 **Milk Group** includes all fluid milk products and foods made from milk that retain their calcium content, such as yogurt and cheese. Foods made from milk that have little to no calcium, such as cream cheese, cream, and butter, are not part of the group. Most milk group choices should be fat-free or low-fat. In general, 1 cup of milk or yogurt, 1 1/2 ounces of natural cheese, or 2 ounces of processed cheese can be considered as 1 cup from the milk group.

7 **Oils** include fats from many different plants and from fish that are liquid at room temperature, such as canola, corn, olive, soybean, and sunflower oil. Some foods are naturally high in oils, like nuts, olives, some fish, and avocados. Foods that are mainly oil include mayonnaise, certain salad dressings, and soft margarine.

8 **Discretionary Calorie Allowance** is the remaining amount of calories in a food intake pattern after accounting for the calories needed for all food groups—using forms of foods that are fat-free or low-fat and with no added sugars.

Estimated Daily Calorie Needs

To determine which food intake pattern to use for an individual, the following chart gives an estimate of individual calorie needs. The calorie range for each age/sex group is based on physical activity level, from sedentary to active.

	Calorie Range	
Children	Sedentary ⟶	Active
2–3 years	1,000 ⟶	1,400
Females		
4–8 years	1,200 ⟶	1,800
9–13	1,600 ⟶	2,200
14–18	1,800 ⟶	2,400
19–30	2,000 ⟶	2,400
31–50	1,800 ⟶	2,200
51+	1,600 ⟶	2,200
Males		
4–8 years	1,400 ⟶	2,000
9–13	1,800 ⟶	2,600
14–18	2,200 ⟶	3,200
19–30	2,400 ⟶	3,000
31–50	2,200 ⟶	3,000
51+	2,000 ⟶	2,800

Sedentary means a lifestyle that includes only the light physical activity associated with typical day-to-day life.

Active means a lifestyle that includes physical activity equivalent to walking more than 3 miles per day at 3 to 4 miles per hour, in addition to the light physical activity associated with typical day-to-day life.

U.S. Department of Agriculture
Center for Nutrition Policy and Promotion
April 2005

Appendix D2

MyPyramid Food Intake Pattern Calorie Levels

MyPyramid assigns individuals to a calorie level based on their sex, age, and activity level.

The chart below identifies the calorie levels for males and females by age and activity level. Calorie levels are provided for each year of childhood, from 2-18 years, and for adults in 5-year increments.

	MALES				FEMALES		
Activity level	Sedentary*	Mod. active*	Active*	Activity level	Sedentary*	Mod. active*	Active*
AGE				AGE			
2	1000	1000	1000	2	1000	1000	1000
3	1000	1400	1400	3	1000	1200	1400
4	1200	1400	1600	4	1200	1400	1400
5	1200	1400	1600	5	1200	1400	1600
6	1400	1600	1800	6	1200	1400	1600
7	1400	1600	1800	7	1200	1600	1800
8	1400	1600	2000	8	1400	1600	1800
9	1600	1800	2000	9	1400	1600	1800
10	1600	1800	2200	10	1400	1800	2000
11	1800	2000	2200	11	1600	1800	2000
12	1800	2200	2400	12	1600	2000	2200
13	2000	2200	2600	13	1600	2000	2200
14	2000	2400	2800	14	1800	2000	2400
15	2200	2600	3000	15	1800	2000	2400
16	2400	2800	3200	16	1800	2000	2400
17	2400	2800	3200	17	1800	2000	2400
18	2400	2800	3200	18	1800	2000	2400
19-20	2600	2800	3000	19-20	2000	2200	2400
21-25	2400	2800	3000	21-25	2000	2200	2400
26-30	2400	2600	3000	26-30	1800	2000	2400
31-35	2400	2600	3000	31-35	1800	2000	2200
36-40	2400	2600	2800	36-40	1800	2000	2200
41-45	2200	2600	2800	41-45	1800	2000	2200
46-50	2200	2400	2800	46-50	1800	2000	2200
51-55	2200	2400	2800	51-55	1600	1800	2200
56-60	2200	2400	2600	56-60	1600	1800	2200
61-65	2000	2400	2600	61-65	1600	1800	2000
66-70	2000	2200	2600	66-70	1600	1800	2000
71-75	2000	2200	2600	71-75	1600	1800	2000
76 and up	2000	2200	2400	76 and up	1600	1800	2000

*Calorie levels are based on the Estimated Energy Requirements (EER) and activity levels from the Institute of Medicine Dietary Reference Intakes Macronutrients Report, 2002.
SEDENTARY = less than 30 minutes a day of moderate physical activity in addition to daily activities.
MOD. ACTIVE = at least 30 minutes up to 60 minutes a day of moderate physical activity in addition to daily activities.
ACTIVE = 60 or more minutes a day of moderate physical activity in addition to daily activities.

United StatesDepartment of Agriculture
Center for Nutrition Policy and Promotion
April 2005
CNPP-XX

Appendix E1

Health Consequences of Eating Disorders

- Eating disorders are serious, potentially life-threatening conditions that affect a person's emotional and physical health.

- Eating disorders are not just a "fad" or a "phase." People do not just "catch" an eating disorder for a period of time. They are real, complex, and devastating conditions that can have serious consequences for health, productivity, and relationships.

- People struggling with an eating disorder need to seek professional help. The earlier a person with an eating disorder seeks treatment, the greater the likelihood of physical and emotional recovery.

Health Consequences of Anorexia Nervosa: In anorexia nervosa's cycle of self-starvation, the body is denied the essential nutrients it needs to function normally. Thus, the body is forced to slow down all of its processes to conserve energy, resulting in serious medical consequences:

- Abnormally slow heart rate and low blood pressure, which mean that the heart muscle is changing. The risk for heart failure rises as the heart rate and blood pressure levels sink lower and lower.

- Reduction of bone density (osteoporosis), which results in dry, brittle bones.

- Muscle loss and weakness.

- Severe dehydration, which can result in kidney failure.

- Fainting, fatigue, and overall weakness.

- Dry hair and skin; hair loss is common.

- Growth of a downy layer of hair called lanugo all over the body, including the face, in an effort to keep the body warm.

Health Consequences of Bulimia Nervosa: The recurrent binge-and-purge cycles of bulimia can affect the entire digestive system and can lead to electrolyte and chemical imbalances in the body that affect the heart and other major organ functions. Some of the health consequences of bulimia nervosa include:

- Electrolyte imbalances that can lead to irregular heartbeats and possibly heart failure and death. Electrolyte imbalance is caused by dehydration and loss of potassium, sodium and chloride from the body as a result of purging behaviors.

- Potential for gastric rupture during periods of bingeing.

- Inflammation and possible rupture of the esophagus from frequent vomiting.

- Tooth decay and staining from stomach acids released during frequent vomiting.

- Chronic irregular bowel movements and constipation as a result of laxative abuse.

- Peptic ulcers and pancreatitis.

Health Consequences of Binge Eating Disorder: Binge eating disorder often results in many of the same health risks associated with clinical obesity. Some of the potential health consequences of binge eating disorder include:

- High blood pressure.

- High cholesterol levels.

- Heart disease as a result of elevated triglyceride levels.

- Type II diabetes mellitus.

- Gallbladder disease.

Appendix E2

The Role of the Educator:
Faculty and Student Guidelines for Meeting With and Referring Students Who May Have Eating Disorders

by: Michael Levine, PhD and Linda Smolak, PhD

1. No matter how strong your suspicion that a student has an eating disorder, do not make a decision without first speaking privately with the student. If possible, select a time to talk when you will not feel rushed. Ensure sufficient time and try to prevent interruptions.

2. Roommates or friends should select the person who has the best rapport with the student to do the talking. Unless the situation is an emergency or otherwise very negative for many people, confrontation by a critical group without professional guidance should be avoided.

3. In a direct and non-punitive manner, indicate to the student all the specific observations that have aroused your concern. Allow the student to respond. If the student discloses information about problems, listen carefully, with empathy, and non-judgmentally.

4. Throughout the conversation, communicate care, concern, and a desire to talk about problems. Your responsibility is not diagnosis or therapy, it is the development of a compassionate and forthright conversation that ultimately helps a student in trouble find understanding, support, and the proper therapeutic resources.

5. If the information you receive is compelling, communicate to the student:

   • Your tentative sense that he or she might have an eating disorder.

   • Your conviction that the matter clearly needs to be evaluated.

   • Your understanding that participation in school, sports, or other activities will not be jeopardized unless health has been compromised to the point where such participation is dangerous.

6. Avoid an argument or battle of wills. Repeat the evidence, your concern, and if warranted your conviction that something must be done. Terminate the conversation if it is going nowhere or if either party becomes too upset. This impasse suggests the need for consultation from a professional.

7. Throughout the process of detection, referral, and recovery, the focus should be on the person feeling healthy and functioning effectively, not weight, shape, or morality.

8. Do not intentionally or unintentionally become the student's therapist, savior, or victim. Attempts to "moralize," develop therapeutic plans, closely monitor the person's eating, adjust one's life around the eating disorder, or cover for the person are not helpful.

9. Be knowledgeable about community resources to which the student can be referred. In discussing the utility of these resources, emphasize to the student that, since eating problems are very hard to overcome on one's own, past unsuccessful attempts are not indicative of lack of effort or moral failure.

10. Faculty should arrange for some type of follow-up contact with the student. If you are often involved with students with eating disorders, consultation with a professional who specializes in eating disorders may be needed.

Appendix E3

The Role of the Educator:
Some "Don'ts" for Educators and Others Concerned About a Person with an Eating Disorder

By: Michael Levine, PhD and Linda Smolak, PhD

1. Don't cast a net of awe and wonder around the existence of an eating disorder. Keep the focus on the reality that eating disorders result in:

   Inefficiency in the fulfillment of academic, familial, occupational, and other responsibilities.

   Misery in the form of food and weight obsession, anxiety about control, guilt, helplessness, hopelessness, and extreme mood swings.

   Alienation in the form of social anxiety, social withdrawal, secrecy, mistrust of others, and self-absorption.

   Disturbance of self and others through loss of control over dieting, body image, eating, emotions, and decisions.

2. Don't oversimplify. Avoid thinking or saying things such as "Well, eating disorders are just an addiction like alcoholism," or "All you have to do is start accepting yourself as you are."

3. Don't imply that bulimia nervosa, because it is often associated with "normal weight," is somehow less serious than anorexia nervosa.

4. Don't be judgmental, e.g., don't tell the person that what they are doing is "sick" or "stupid" or "self-destructive."

5. Don't give advice about weight loss, exercise, or appearance.

6. Don't confront the person as part of a group of people, all of whom are firing accusations at the person at once.

7. Don't diagnose: keep the focus on IMAD (inefficiency, misery, alienation, disturbance) and the ways that the behaviors are impacting the person's life and well-being.

8. Don't become the person's therapist, savior, or victim. In this regard, do not "promise to keep this a secret no matter what."

9. Don't get into an argument or a battle of wills. If the person denies having a problem, simply and calmly:

   - Repeat what you have observed, i.e., your evidence for a problem.
   - Repeat your concern about the person's health and well-being.
   - Repeat your conviction that the circumstance should at least be evaluated by a counselor or therapist.
   - End the conversation if it is going nowhere or if either party becomes too upset. This impasse suggests that the person seeking help needs to consult a professional.
   - Take any actions necessary for you to carry out your responsibilities or to protect yourself.
   - If possible, leave the door open for further conversations.

10. Don't be inactive during an emergency: If the person is throwing up several times per day, or passing out, or complaining of chest pain, or is suicidal, get professional help immediately.

Appendix E4

How to Help a Friend with Eating and Body Image Issues

If you are reading this handout, chances are you are concerned about the eating habits, weight, or body image of someone you care about. We understand that this can be a very difficult and scary time for you. Let us assure you that you are doing a great thing by looking for more information! This list may not tell you everything you need to know about what to do in your specific situation, but it will give you some helpful ideas on what to do to help your friend.

Learn as much as you can about eating disorders. Read books, articles, and brochures.

Know the differences between facts and myths about weight, nutrition, and exercise. Knowing the facts will help you reason against any inaccurate ideas that your friend may be using as excuses to maintain their disordered eating patterns.

Be honest. Talk openly and honestly about your concerns with the person who is struggling with eating or body image problems. Avoiding it or ignoring it won't help!

Be caring, but be firm. Caring about your friend does not mean being manipulated by them. Your friend must be responsible for their actions and the consequences of those actions. Avoid making rules, promises, or expectations that you cannot or will not uphold. For example, "I promise not to tell anyone." Or, "If you do this one more time I'll never talk to you again."

Compliment your friend's wonderful personality, successes, or accomplishments. Remind your friend that "true beauty" is not simply skin deep.

Be a good role model in regard to sensible eating, exercise, and self-acceptance.

Tell someone. It may seem difficult to know when, if at all, to tell someone else about your concerns. Addressing body image or eating problems in their beginning stages offers your friend the best chance for working through these issues and becoming healthy again. Don't wait until the situation is so severe that your friend's life is in danger. Your friend needs as much support and understanding as possible.

Remember that you cannot force someone to seek help, change their habits, or adjust their attitudes. You will make important progress in honestly sharing your concerns, providing support, and knowing where to go for more information! People struggling with anorexia, bulimia, or binge eating disorder do need professional help.

There is help available and there is hope!

Appendix E5

What Should I Say?
Tips for Talking to a Friend Who May Be Struggling with an Eating Disorder

If you are worried about your friend's eating behaviors or attitudes, it is important to express your concerns in a loving and supportive way. It is also necessary to discuss your worries early on, rather than waiting until your friend has endured many of the damaging physical and emotional effects of eating disorders. In a private and relaxed setting, talk to your friend in a calm and caring way about the specific things you have seen or felt that have caused you to worry.

What to Say—Step by Step

Set a time to talk. Set aside a time for a private, respectful meeting with your friend to discuss your concerns openly and honestly in a caring, supportive way. Make sure you will be some place away from other distractions.

Communicate your concerns. Share your memories of specific times when you felt concerned about your friend's eating or exercise behaviors. Explain that you think these things may indicate that there could be a problem that needs professional attention.

Ask your friend to explore these concerns with a counselor, doctor, nutritionist, or other health professional who is knowledgeable about eating issues. If you feel comfortable doing so, offer to help your friend make an appointment or accompany your friend on their first visit.

Avoid conflicts or a battle of the wills with your friend. If your friend refuses to acknowledge that there is a problem, or any reason for you to be concerned, restate your feelings and the reasons for them and leave yourself open and available as a supportive listener.

Avoid placing shame, blame, or guilt on your friend regarding their actions or attitudes. Do not use accusatory "you" statements like, "You just need to eat." Or, "You are acting irresponsibly." Instead, use "I" statements. For example: "I'm concerned about you because you refuse to eat breakfast or lunch." Or, "It makes me afraid to hear you vomiting."

Avoid giving simple solutions. For example, "If you'd just stop, then everything would be fine!"

Express your continued support. Remind your friend that you care and want your friend to be healthy and happy.

After talking with your friend, if you are still concerned with their health and safety, find a trusted adult or medical professional to talk to. This is probably a challenging time for both of you. It could be helpful for you, as well as your friend, to discuss your concerns and seek assistance and support from a professional.

Appendix E6

What Can You Do to Help Prevent Eating Disorders?

* Learn all you can about anorexia nervosa, bulimia nervosa, and binge eating disorder. Genuine awareness will help you avoid judgmental or mistaken attitudes about food, weight, body shape, and eating disorders.

* Discourage the idea that a particular diet, weight, or body size will automatically lead to happiness and fulfillment.

* Choose to challenge the false belief that thinness and weight loss are great, while body fat and weight gain are horrible or indicate laziness, worthlessness, or immorality.

* Avoid categorizing foods as "good/safe" vs. "bad/dangerous." Remember, we all need to eat a balanced variety of foods.

* Decide to avoid judging others and yourself on the basis of body weight or shape. Turn off the voices in your head that tell you that a person's body weight says anything about their character, personality, or value as a person.

* Avoid conveying an attitude that says, "I will like you better if you lose weight, or don't eat so much, etc."

* Become a critical viewer of the media and its messages about self-esteem and body image. Talk back to the television when you hear a comment or see an image that promotes thinness at all costs. Rip out (or better yet, write to the editor about) advertisements or articles in your magazines that make you feel bad about your body shape or size.

* If you think someone has an eating disorder, express your concerns in a forthright, caring manner. Gently but firmly encourage the person to seek trained professional help.

* Be a model of healthy self-esteem and body image. Recognize that others pay attention and learn from the way you talk about yourself and your body. Choose to talk about yourself with respect and appreciation. Choose to value yourself based on your goals, accomplishments, talents, and character. Avoid letting the way you feel about your body weight and shape determine the course of your day. Embrace the natural diversity of human bodies and celebrate your body's unique shape and size.

* Support local and national nonprofit eating disorders organizations — like the National Eating Disorders Association — by volunteering your time or giving a tax-deductible donation.

 Don't Weigh Your Self-Esteem, It's What's Inside That Counts!

Appendix F

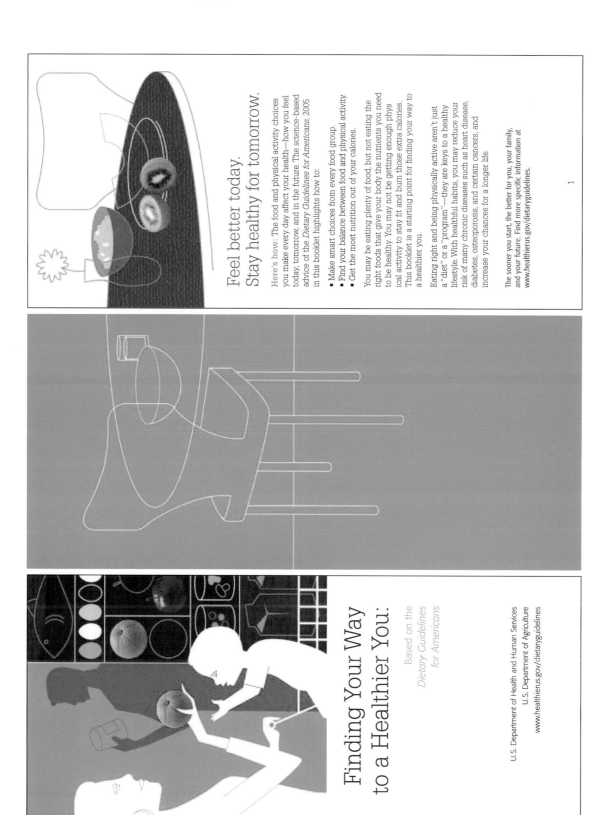

Feel better today.
Stay healthy for tomorrow.

Here's how: The food and physical activity choices you make every day affect your health—how you feel today, tomorrow, and in the future. The science-based advice of the *Dietary Guidelines for Americans, 2005* in this booklet highlights how to:

- Make smart choices from every food group.
- Find your balance between food and physical activity.
- Get the most nutrition out of your calories.

You may be eating plenty of food, but not eating the right foods that give your body the nutrients you need to be healthy. You may not be getting enough physical activity to stay fit and burn those extra calories. This booklet is a starting point for finding your way to a healthier you.

Eating right and being physically active aren't just a "diet" or a "program"—they are keys to a healthy lifestyle. With healthful habits, you may reduce your risk of many chronic diseases such as heart disease, diabetes, osteoporosis, and certain cancers, and increase your chances for a longer life.

The sooner you start, the better for you, your family, and your future. Find more specific information at www.healthierus.gov/dietaryguidelines.

1

Finding Your Way
to a Healthier You:

Based on the
*Dietary Guidelines
for Americans*

U.S. Department of Health and Human Services
U.S. Department of Agriculture
www.healthierus.gov/dietaryguidelines

Find your balance between food and physical activity.

Becoming a healthier you isn't just about eating healthy—it's also about physical activity. Regular physical activity is important for your overall health and fitness. It also helps you control body weight by balancing the calories you take in as food with the calories you expend each day.

- Be physically active for at least 30 minutes most days of the week.
- Increasing the intensity or the amount of time that you are physically active can have even greater health benefits and may be needed to control body weight. About 60 minutes a day may be needed to prevent weight gain.
- Children and teenagers should be physically active for 60 minutes every day, or most every day.

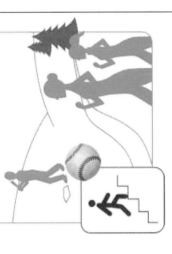

CONSIDER THIS:

If you eat 100 more food calories a day than you burn, you'll gain about 1 pound in a month. That's about 10 pounds in a year. The bottom line is that to lose weight, it's important to reduce calories and increase physical activity.

4

Mix up your choices within each food group.

Focus on fruits. Eat a variety of fruits—whether fresh, frozen, canned, or dried—rather than fruit juice for most of your fruit choices. For a 2,000-calorie diet, you will need 2 cups of fruit each day (for example, 1 small banana, 1 large orange, and ¼ cup of dried apricots or peaches).

Vary your veggies. Eat more dark green veggies, such as broccoli, kale, and other dark leafy greens; orange veggies, such as carrots, sweetpotatoes, pumpkin, and winter squash; and beans and peas, such as pinto beans, kidney beans, black beans, garbanzo beans, split peas, and lentils.

Get your calcium-rich foods. Get 3 cups of low-fat or fat-free milk—or an equivalent amount of low-fat yogurt and/or low-fat cheese (1½ ounces of cheese equals 1 cup of milk)—every day. For kids aged 2 to 8, it's 2 cups of milk. If you don't or can't consume milk, choose lactose-free milk products and/or calcium-fortified foods and beverages.

Make half your grains whole. Eat at least 3 ounces of whole-grain cereals, breads, crackers, rice, or pasta every day. One ounce is about 1 slice of bread, 1 cup of breakfast cereal, or ½ cup of cooked rice or pasta. Look to see that grains such as wheat, rice, oats, or corn are referred to as "whole" in the list of ingredients.

Go lean with protein. Choose lean meats and poultry. Bake it, broil it, or grill it. And vary your protein choices—with more fish, beans, peas, nuts, and seeds.

Know the limits on fats, salt, and sugars. Read the Nutrition Facts label on foods. Look for foods low in saturated fats and *trans* fats. Choose and prepare foods and beverages with little salt (sodium) and/or added sugars (caloric sweeteners).

3

Make smart choices from every food group.

The best way to give your body the balanced nutrition it needs is by eating a variety of nutrient-packed foods every day. Just be sure to stay within your daily calorie needs.

A healthy eating plan is one that:
- Emphasizes fruits, vegetables, whole grains, and fat-free or low-fat milk and milk products.
- Includes lean meats, poultry, fish, beans, eggs, and nuts.
- Is low in saturated fats, *trans* fats, cholesterol, salt (sodium), and added sugars.

DON'T GIVE IN WHEN YOU EAT OUT AND ARE ON THE GO

It's important to make smart food choices and watch portion sizes wherever you are—at the grocery store, at work, in your favorite restaurant, or running errands. Try these tips:

- At the store, plan ahead by buying a variety of nutrient-rich foods for meals and snacks throughout the week.
- When grabbing lunch, have a sandwich on whole-grain bread and choose low-fat/fat-free milk, water, or other drinks without added sugars.
- In a restaurant, opt for steamed, grilled, or broiled dishes instead of those that are fried or sautéed.
- On a long commute or shopping trip, pack some fresh fruit, cut-up vegetables, string cheese sticks, or a handful of unsalted nuts—to help you avoid impulsive, less healthful snack choices.

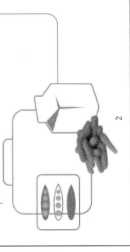

2

NUTRITION:
To know the facts…

Most packaged foods have a Nutrition Facts label. For a healthier you, use this tool to make smart food choices quickly and easily. Try these tips:

- Keep these low: saturated fats, *trans* fats, cholesterol, and sodium.
- Get enough of these: potassium, fiber, vitamins A and C, calcium, and iron.
- Use the % Daily Value (DV) column when possible: 5% DV or less is low, 20% DV or more is high.

Check servings and calories. Look at the serving size and how many servings you are actually consuming. If you double the servings you eat, you double the calories and nutrients, including the % DVs.

Make your calories count. Look at the calories on the label and compare them with what nutrients you are also getting to decide whether the food is worth eating. When one serving of a single food item has over 400 calories per serving, it is high in calories.

Don't sugarcoat it. Since sugars contribute calories with few, if any, nutrients, look for foods and beverages low in added sugars. Read the ingredient list and make sure that added sugars are not one of the first few ingredients. Some names for added sugars (caloric sweeteners) include sucrose, glucose, high fructose corn syrup, corn syrup, maple syrup, and fructose.

Know your fats. Look for foods low in saturated fats, *trans* fats, and cholesterol to help reduce the risk of heart disease (5% DV or less is low, 20% DV or more is high). Most of the fats you eat should be polyunsaturated and monounsaturated fats. Keep total fat intake between 20% to 35% of calories.

Reduce sodium (salt), increase potassium. Research shows that eating less than 2,300 milligrams of sodium (about 1 tsp of salt) per day may reduce the risk of high blood pressure. Most of the sodium people eat comes from processed foods, not from the saltshaker. Also look for foods high in potassium, which counteracts some of sodium's effects on blood pressure.

…use the label.

Nutrition Facts

Serving Size 1 cup (228g)
Servings Per Container 2

Amount Per Serving		
Calories 260	Calories from Fat 110	
		% Daily Value*
Total Fat 12g		**18%**
Saturated Fat 3g		**15%**
Trans Fat 3g		
Cholesterol 30mg		**10%**
Sodium 470mg		**20%**
Potassium 700mg		**20%**
Total Carbohydrate 31g		**10%**
Dietary Fiber 0g		**0%**
Sugars 5g		
Protein 5g		
Vitamin A		**4%**
Vitamin C		**2%**
Calcium		**20%**
Iron		**4%**

* Percent Daily Values are based on a 2,000 calorie diet. Your Daily Values may be higher or lower depending on your calorie needs:

	Calories	2,000	2,500
Total Fat	Less than	65g	80g
Sat Fat	Less than	20g	25g
Cholesterol	Less than	300mg	300mg
Sodium	Less than	2,400mg	2,400mg
Total Carbohydrate		300g	375g
Dietary Fiber		25g	30g

Start here

Check calories

Quick guide to % DV
5% or less is low
20% or more is high

Limit these

Get enough of these

Footnote

7

Get the most nutrition out of your calories.

There is a right number of calories for you to eat each day. This number depends on your age, activity level, and whether you're trying to gain, maintain, or lose weight.* You could use up the entire amount on a few high-calorie items, but chances are you won't get the full range of vitamins and nutrients your body needs to be healthy.

Choose the most nutritionally rich foods you can from each food group each day—those packed with vitamins, minerals, fiber, and other nutrients but lower in calories. Pick foods like fruits, vegetables, whole grains, and fat-free or low-fat milk and milk products more often.

* 2,000 calories is the value used as a general reference on the food label. But you can calculate your number at www.healthierus.gov/dietaryguidelines.

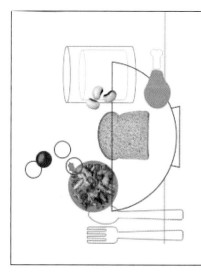

5

6

Play it safe with food.

Know how to prepare, handle, and store food safely to keep you and your family safe:

- Clean hands, food-contact surfaces, fruits, and vegetables. To avoid spreading bacteria to other foods, meat and poultry should *not* be washed or rinsed.
- Separate raw, cooked, and ready-to-eat foods while shopping, preparing, or storing.
- Cook meat, poultry, and fish to safe internal temperatures to kill microorganisms.
- Chill perishable foods promptly and thaw foods properly.

180°F — Whole poultry
170°F — Poultry breasts
165°F — Stuffing, ground poultry, reheat leftovers
160°F — Meats (medium), egg dishes, pork, and ground meats
145°F — Beef steaks, roasts, veal, lamb (medium rare)
140°F — Hold hot foods

DANGER ZONE

40°F — Refrigerator temperatures

0°F — Freezer temperatures

About alcohol.

If you choose to drink alcohol, do so in moderation. Moderate drinking means up to 1 drink a day for women and up to 2 drinks for men. Twelve ounces of regular beer, 5 ounces of wine, or 1½ ounces of 80-proof distilled spirits count as a drink for purposes of explaining moderation. Remember that alcoholic beverages have calories but are low in nutritional value.

Generally, anything more than moderate drinking can be harmful to your health. And some people, or people in certain situations, shouldn't drink at all. If you have questions or concerns, talk to your doctor or healthcare provider.

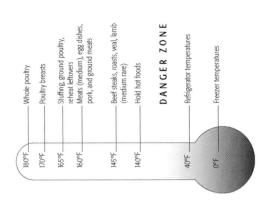

These are the basic guidelines for eating a healthy diet and being physically active. For more information about the food groups and nutrition values, or to pick up some new ideas on physical activity, go to www.healthierus.gov/dietaryguidelines.

This booklet, as well as *Dietary Guidelines for Americans*, 2005, 6th Edition, may be viewed and downloaded from the Internet at www.healthierus.gov/dietaryguidelines.

To purchase printed copies of this booklet (Stock Number 001-000-04718-3), call the U.S. Government Printing Office toll-free at (866) 512-1800, or access the GPO Online Bookstore at http://bookstore.gpo.gov.

To purchase printed copies of the complete 80-page *Dietary Guidelines for Americans*, 2005 (Stock Number 001-000-04719-1), call the U.S. Government Printing Office at (866) 512-1800, or access the GPO Online Bookstore at http://bookstore.gpo.gov.

HHS Publication number: HHS-ODPHP-2005-01-DGA-B
USDA Publication number: Home and Garden Bulletin No. 232-CP

USDA

ISBN 0-16-072399-X

90000

9 780160 723995

Adenosine Triphosphate (ATP): The form of energy the body uses at a cellular level.

Adequate Intake (AI): The amount of a nutrient believed to cover the needs of almost all individuals in the group. This designation implies that further research is needed and that this value is based on limited data.

Adipose Tissue Triglyceride: Triglyceride stored in the adipose tissue.

Aerobic Metabolism: Also known as oxidative phosphorylation. An energy system that generates ATP from the breakdown of carbohydrates, fats, or proteins. This system can supply ATP on a fairly limitless basis.

American Dietetic Association (ADA): A leading professional organization that governs the practice of nutrition and dietetics. A credible source for food and nutrition information (www.eatright.org).

Amino Acid: The smallest unit of a protein.

Anaerobic Glycolysis: An energy system that generates ATP fairly rapidly from the breakdown of glucose.

Anorexia Athletica: Not an official eating disorder listed in the DSM-IV, but is common in athletes who use energy restriction and/or excessive exercise to maintain a low body weight in an attempt to enhance performance.

Anorexia Nervosa: A medical condition characterized by an intense fear of becoming fat and a refusal to maintain a healthy body weight.

Antioxidant: Compound that protects cells from free radical damage.

Bioelectrical Impedance Analysis: A body-composition assessment technique that uses an electrical current to measure resistance and then estimate percent body fat.

Biological Value: Compares the amount of nitrogen absorbed from the food with that retained in the body for maintenance and growth.

Body Mass Index: A weight-for-height standard that is related to body-fat content.

Bulimia Nervosa: A medical condition characterized by consuming large quantities of food (binging) followed by a compensatory behavior to prevent body weight gain.

Glossary

Carbohydrate Loading: A technique that begins about a week before an endurance event with the purpose of maximizing glycogen stores. It is characterized by a few days of glycogen depletion with exercise and low to moderate carbohydrate intake followed by glycogen repletion with tapered exercise and high carbohydrate intake.

Case Studies: Published observations on a person or group of people.

Chylomicron: A lipoprotein that transports dietary triglycerides.

Chyme: A mixture of partially digested food and stomach secretions.

Complete Protein: A protein that contains all nine essential amino acids.

Dietary Approaches to Stop Hypertension (DASH): Research-based guidelines showing that diets moderate in sodium and rich in fruits and vegetables that include low-fat dairy and lean protein may be effective in improving blood pressure (www.dashdiet.org).

Dietary Guidelines for Americans: Guidelines published by the USDA and the Department of Health and Human Services (www.health.gov/dietaryguidelines) that are designed to meet nutrient requirements, promote health, and prevent disease in people over the age of two.

Dietary Reference Intakes (DRIs): Developed by the Food and Nutrition Board of the Institute of Medicine in the United States and Health Canada. Umbrella term for nutrient recommendations. Includes Recommended Dietary Allowance (RDA), Adequate Intake (AI), Estimated Energy Requirement (EER), and Upper Level (UL).

Dietary Supplement Health and Education Act (DSHEA): Legally defined a dietary supplement as a product (other than tobacco) added to the total diet that contains at least one of the following: a vitamin, mineral, amino acid, herb, botanical, or concentrate, metabolite, constituent, or extract of such ingredients or combination of any ingredient described previously.

Digestion: The process of mechanically and chemically breaking down larger consumed food molecules to smaller particles that can be absorbed across the wall of the small intestine.

Dipeptide: Two amino acids joined together.

Disaccharides: Two monosaccharides joined together (i.e., lactose, maltose, sucrose).

Diverticulosis: A medical condition characterized by pockets forming in the large intestine. These pockets generally come from years of pressure from straining to pass stool.

Dual Energy X-Ray Absorptiometry (DXA): A body-composition assessment technique that uses X-rays to measure bone density and percent body fat.

Dyslipidemia: A term to describe abnormal serum lipoproteins, especially elevated total cholesterol and LDL cholesterol, and lowered HDL cholesterol.

Eating Disorders Not Otherwise Specified (EDNOS): A category of eating disorders that describes individuals who do not meet all, but have some, of the specific criteria for anorexia nervosa or bulimia nervosa.

Electrolyte: A substance that separates into ions in solution and, therefore, conducts an electrical current; include sodium, chloride, and potassium.

Energy Balance: Energy (calories) consumed equals energy (calories) used or burned. Body weight is stable in this condition.

Energy Expenditure Due to Physical Activity (EEPA): Any movement of the body above rest, including purposeful exercise, representing 15-30% of the total daily energy expenditure in most individuals.

Energy Nutrients: Nutrients that provide calories (or energy) (e.g., carbohydrates, proteins, and fats).

Enriched Foods: Some of the nutrients lost with processing are added back to the foods.

Epidemiological Studies: Studies that report associations or correlations between two variables, generally on larger populations.

Essential Amino Acid: Any of the nine amino acids that must be consumed in the diet because the body cannot synthesize them.

Estimated Energy Requirement (EER): Used to estimate the energy needs of an average person using gender, height, weight, age, and physical-activity level.

Euhydration: A state of adequate fluid balance.

Evidence-Based Medicine: The conscientious, explicit, and judicious use of current best evidence in making decisions about the care of individual patients.

Experimental Studies: Research studies or projects that use the scientific process or method to test a research question or hypothesis.

Fat-Free Mass: Tissue absent of all extractable fat. Often used interchangeably with lean body mass, although not technically equivalent.

Fat-Soluble Vitamins: Vitamins that dissolve in fat; vitamins A, D, E, and K.

Fatty Acid: The simplest unit of a lipid; contains long chains of carbon molecules bound to each other and to hydrogen atoms.

Female Athlete Triad: Term is used to bring together three related conditions: disordered eating (usually a low energy intake), amenorrhea, and osteopenia or osteoporosis (low bone density).

Fiber: A chain of glucose molecules that the human body cannot break down (digest) due to lack of appropriate enzymes.

Food Label: A result of the Nutrition Labeling and Education Act of 1990. Displays nutrient content of a food product. Regulated by the United States Food and Drug Administration (FDA; www.fda.gov).

Fortified Foods: Foods that have added nutrients that may not naturally occur in the product.

Four-Compartment Body-Composition Model: Model that separates the body components into fat, muscle, bone, and water.

Gastrointestinal Reflux Disease (GERD): A medical condition where the acidic chyme from the stomach enters the esophagus.

Glucogenic Amino Acid: An amino acid that can be converted to glucose via gluconeogenesis.

Gluconeogenesis: A process of synthesizing glucose from noncarbohydrate precursors.

Glucose: The usable form of carbohydrate in the body.

Glycemic Index: A rating system used to describe a food's potential to raise blood glucose and insulin levels. The incremental area under the plasma glucose curve in response to 50 g of available carbohydrate, in the fasted state, compared to a reference food (glucose or white bread).

Glycemic Load: The quantity of carbohydrate in food multiplied by the glycemic index of the food.

Glycogen: The storage form of carbohydrate in the human body; found in both the liver and in skeletal muscle.

Health Claims: Statements approved for use by the FDA that describe the relationship between a nutrient and a specific disease or health-related condition.

Hyperlipidemia: A term to describe elevated serum lipoproteins, especially total cholesterol and LDL cholesterol.

Hypohydration: A state of low levels of body water due to intake being less than loss; often called dehydration.

Hyponatremia: A general medical condition meaning low serum sodium. Exercise-associated hyponatremia is specific to athletes and usually occurs with long-duration endurance events.

Ideal/Desirable Body Weight: A body weight associated with the lowest risk of death; may not be practical for all individuals.

Incomplete Protein: A protein that lacks one or more essential amino acids.

Intramuscular Triglyceride: Triglyceride stored within the skeletal muscle.

Ketoacidosis: A medical condition characterized by excessive ketone levels in the blood, resulting in an acidic state and potential tissue damage.

Kilocalorie (kcal): The amount of heat required to raise the temperature of one kilogram of water by one degree Celsius. Common term used to describe energy content of food or energy expended.

Lacto-ovo-vegetarian: A person who consumes plants, dairy foods, and eggs.

Lacto-vegetarian: A person who consumes plants and dairy foods.

Lean Body Mass: Contains a small percentage of essential fat; generally refers to muscle (skeletal and smooth), bone, and water. Often used interchangeably with fat-free mass.

Lipoprotein: Vehicle that transports lipids through the lymph and circulatory systems. Contains a lipid center surrounded by a protein shell.

Macronutrients: Nutrients required in larger quantities, including carbohydrates, lipids, proteins, and water.

Megadose: Nutrient intake beyond those needed to prevent deficiency; at least 10 times the estimated requirement.

Meta-Analysis: Similar to a review article, except the authors take data from other primary research articles and statistically reanalyze it to put the results on a level playing field.

Metabolism: A sum of all the chemical reactions in the body.

Micronutrients: Nutrients required in small or trace amounts, including vitamins and minerals.

Monosaccharide: The simplest unit of a carbohydrate (i.e., glucose, fructose, and galactose).

Monounsaturated Fatty Acids: Fatty acids with double bonds between some of the carbons and, hence, room to add more hydrogen molecules. Monounsaturated fats have one double bond; common examples include olive oil and canola oil.

MyPyramid: A Food Guidance System designed and supported by the United States Department of Agriculture (USDA; www.mypyramod.gov).

National Weight Control Registry: Created in 1994, it is the largest research investigation of successful weight-loss maintenance, containing data on more than 5,000 individuals who have lost significant amounts of weight and who have maintained that weight loss for extended amounts of time (www.nwcr.ws/).

Nitrogen Balance: A physiological state in which dietary nitrogen consumed equals nitrogen output. The classical method for determining dietary protein requirements.

Nutrient Content Claims: Claims approved by the FDA that define quantities of nutrients in a product.

Nutrition: The scientific study of the relationship between food and health and disease.

Office of Dietary Supplements: An office of the National Institutes of Health. A reliable source for information about dietary supplements (ods.od.nih.gov).

Omega-3 Fatty Acid: An essential fatty acid (it must be consumed in the diet). Found in fatty fish, flax seed, and certain nuts (e.g., walnuts and almonds).

Omega-6 Fatty Acid: An essential fatty acid (it must be consumed in the diet). Found in many vegetable oils.

Peer-Reviewed Journal Article: An article that has gone through a formal review process by other experts in the field. This process ensures that published research studies have been scrutinized by impartial experts for the soundness of the research methods utilized, and that the conclusions of the authors are supported by their research findings.

Phosphocreatine System: An energy system that produces ATP rapidly, but has a limited production capacity.

Phytochemicals: Biologically active compounds found in plants that may play a role in health promotion or the prevention of disease.

Plethysmography: A body-composition assessment technique that uses air displacement to measure body volume and then estimate percent body fat.

Polypeptide: Many amino acids joined together.

Polysaccharides: Long chains of monosaccharides (e.g., starch, fiber, and glycogen).

Polyunsaturated Fatty Acids: Fatty acids with double bonds between some of the carbons and, hence, room to add more hydrogen molecules. Polyunsaturated fatty acids have more than one double bond and are commonly found in many vegetable oils.

Primary Research Article: Published results of a research study or experiment.

Protein Digestibility-Corrected Amino Acid Score (PDCAAS): The USDA's official method for determining protein quality, accounting for both amino acid composition and digestibility.

PubMed: A database of biomedical articles from the National Library of Medicine database (www.pubmed.gov).

Recommended Dietary Allowance (RDA): Set to meet the needs of almost all (97-98%) individuals in the reference group.

Registered Dietitian: A legal credential governed by the Commission on Dietetic Registration of the American Dietetic Association. A specialized college degree, supervised practice experience, and passing of a national examination are required to earn the credential.

Resting Metabolic Rate (RMR): The amount of energy the body expends just to maintain itself at rest. It is largest component (60-75%) of the total daily energy expenditure. Also known as resting energy expenditure.

Review Article: A summary of previous studies that have been published up to that point in time.

Saturated Fatty Acids: Fatty acids where the carbon molecules are saturated with hydrogen. They tend to be solid at room temperature and are associated with an increased risk of developing hyperlipidemia when overconsumed.

Short-Term Fatigue: Occurs when exercise intensity rises to levels that disturb the body's ability to break down and transport the carbon, hydrogen, and oxygen molecules in macronutrients.

Skinfold Assessment: A body-composition assessment technique that uses a caliper to measure the thickness of subcutaneous body fat.

Sports Dietetics: The specific practice of using the Nutrition Care Process in counseling athletes and active individuals. These services are provided by a registered dietitian and/or a certified specialist in sports dietetics (CSSD).

Sports Drinks: A term usually used to describe a beverage containing carbohydrate and electrolytes.

Sports Nutrition: The scientific study of the relationship between food and nutrients and athletic performance.

Sports, Cardiovascular, and Wellness Nutrition (SCAN): A dietetics practice group of the American Dietetic Association composed of dietitians who practice in the areas of cardiovascular, sports, and wellness nutrition (www.scandpg.org).

Starch: The storage form of carbohydrate in plants; is abundant in the human diet.

Structure-Function Claims: These claims are not approved by the FDA. Products using these claims must include a disclaimer statement.

Thermic Effect of Food: The energy expended to digest and metabolize food, representing only 5-10% of the total daily energy expenditure.

Three-Compartment Body-Composition Model: Model that separates the body components into fat and lean body mass, with an independent assessment of body water.

Total Daily Energy Expenditure: Energy expended in a 24-hour period.

Trans Fatty Acids: Fatty acids with hydrogen molecules being on opposite sides of the double bonds. This solid vegetable-based compound has great cooking properties, but is associated with an increased risk of developing dyslipidemia when overconsumed.

Triglyceride: A form of lipid in the human diet and the form stored in the human body. A triglyceride contains three fatty acid molecules joined together by a three-carbon alcohol called glycerol.

Tripeptide: Three amino acids joined together.

Two-Compartment Body-Composition Model: Model that separates the body components into fat and lean body mass.

Underwater Weighing: A body-composition assessment technique that uses body density measurements to estimate percent body fat.

Upper Level (UL): The highest amount of a nutrient that when consumed regularly will unlikely result in adverse health effect.

Vegan: A person who consumes only plant foods.

Water-Soluble Vitamins: Vitamins that dissolve in water; includes the B vitamins and vitamin C.

Weight Cycling: The process of continuously losing and gaining weight.

Wheat Flour: Any flour made from wheat; it may contain white flour, unbleached flour, or whole-wheat flour. May also contain fiber.

Whey Protein: The liquid portion of curdled milk that contains a high concentration of branched-chain amino acids (isoleucine, leucine, and valine).

White Flour: Flour that has been refined and bleached. Lacks significant fiber.

Whole-Grain Flour: A nonrefined grain; only the husk is removed. Contains fiber.

American College of Sports Medicine. (2007). ACSM Position Stand: Exercise and Fluid Replacement. *Med Sci Sports Exerc, 39*(2):377-390.

American College of Sports Medicine. (2009). *ACSM's Resource Manual for Guidelines for Exercise Testing and Prescription* (Sixth ed). Philadelphia, PA: Lippincott Williams & Wilkins.

American Dietetic Association. From www.eatright.org

American Psychiatric Association. (1994). Eating Disorders. In *Diagnostic and Statistical Manual of Mental Disorders* (Fourth ed., pp. 539-550). Washington, DC: American Psychiatric Press.

Anderson, J.W. et al. (2005). Soy compared to casein meal-replacement shakes with energy-restricted diets for obese women: Randomized controlled trial. *Metabolism, 56*(2)*, 280-8.*

Benardot, D. (2007). Timing of energy and fluid intake: New concepts for weight control and hydration. *ACSM's Health & Fitness Journal, 11*(4), 13-19.

Bent, S., Padula, A., & Neuhaus, J. (2004). Safety and efficacy of citrus aurantium for weight loss. *Am J Cardiol*, *94*(10), 1359-1361.

Bloomer, R. J., Sforzo, G. A., & Keller, B. A. (2000). Effects of meal form and composition on plasma testosterone, cortisol, and insulin following resistance exercise. *Int J Sport Nutr Exerc Metab, 10*(4), 415-424.

Borsheim, E., Tipton, K. D., Wolf, S. E., & Wolfe, R. R. (2002). Essential amino acids and muscle protein recovery from resistance exercise. *Am J Physiol Endocrinol Metab*, *283*(4), E648-657.

Brandsch, C. & Eder, K. (2002). Effect of L-carnitine on weight loss and body composition of rats fed a hypocaloric diet. *Ann Nutr Metab, 46*(5), 205-210.

Bravata, D. M., Sanders, L., Huang, J., Krumholz, H. M., Olkin, I., & Gardner, C. D. (2003). Efficacy and safety of low-carbohydrate diets: A systematic review. *JAMA, 289*(14), 1837-1850.

Campbell, J. I., Mortensen, A., & Molgaard, P. (2006). Tissue lipid lowering-effect of a traditional Nigerian anti-diabetic infusion of Rauwolfia vomitoria foilage and Citrus aurantium fruit. *J Ethnopharmacol, 104*(3), 379-386.

Centers for Disease Control and Prevention. From www.cdc.gov

Chandler, R. M., Byrne, H. K., Patterson, J. G., & Ivy, J. L. (1994). Dietary supplements affect the anabolic hormones after weight-training exercise. *J Appl Physiol, 76*(2), 839-845.

Chesley, A., MacDougall, J. D., Tarnopolsky, M. A., Atkinson, S. A., & Smith, K. (1992). Changes in human muscle protein synthesis after resistance exercise. *J Appl Physiol, 73*(4), 1383-1388.

Commission on Accreditation for Dietetics Education. From www.eatright.org/cade

ConsumerLab. From www.consumerlab.com

Dansinger, M. L., Gleason, J. A., Griffith, J. L., Selker, H. P., & Schaefer, E. J. (2005). Comparison of the Atkins, Ornish, Weight Watchers, and Zone diets for weight loss and heart disease risk reduction: A randomized trial. *JAMA, 293*(1), 43-53.

Diepvens, K., Kovacs, E. M., Nijs, I. M., Vogels, N., & Westerterp-Plantenga, M. S. (2005). Effect of green tea on resting energy expenditure and substrate oxidation during weight loss in overweight females. *Br J Nutr, 94*(6), 1026-1034.

Diepvens, K., Kovacs, E. M., Vogels, N., & Westerterp-Plantenga, M. S. (2006). Metabolic effects of green tea and of phases of weight loss. *Physiol Behav, 87*(1), 185-191.

Dietary Approaches to Stop Hypertension (DASH). From www.dashdiet.org

Dietary Guidelines for Americans. From www.health.gov/dietaryguidelines

Downs, B. W., Bagchi, M., Subbaraju, G. V., Shara, M. A., Preuss, H. G., & Bagchi, D. (2005). Bioefficacy of a novel calcium-potassium salt of (-)-hydroxycitric acid. *Mutat Res, 579*(1-2), 149-162.

Drapeau, V., Despres, J. P., Bouchard, C., Allard, L., Fournier, G., Leblanc, C., et al. (2004). Modifications in food-group consumption are related to long-term body-weight changes. *Am J Clin Nutr, 80*(1), 29-37.

Dunford, M. (Ed.). (2006). *Sports Nutrition: A Practice Manual for Professionals* (Fourth ed.). Chicago: The American Dietetic Association.

Dunford, M. & Doyle, J. A. (2008). *Nutrition for Sport and Exercise*. Belmont, CA: Thompson Wadsworth.

Foster, G. D., Wyatt, H. R., Hill, J. O., McGuckin, B. G., Brill, C., Mohammed, B. S., et al. (2003). A randomized trial of a low-carbohydrate diet for obesity. *N Engl J Med, 348*(21), 2082-2090.

Gatorade Sports Science Institute. From www.gssiweb.org

Gaullier, J. M., Halse, J., Hoye, K., Kristiansen, K., Fagertun, H., Vik, H., et al. (2005). Supplementation with conjugated linoleic acid for 24 months is well tolerated by and reduces body fat mass in healthy, overweight humans. *J Nutr, 135*(4), 778-784.

Gray, G. & Gray, L. (2002). Evidence-Based Medicine: Applications in Dietetics Practice. *J Am Diet Assoc, 102*, 1263-1272.

Haaz, S., Fontaine, K. R., Cutter, G., Limdi, N., Perumean-Chaney, S., & Allison, D. B. (2006). Citrus aurantium and synephrine alkaloids in the treatment of overweight and obesity: An update. *Obes Rev, 7*(1), 79-88.

Haller, C. A., Benowitz, N. L., & Jacob, P., 3rd. (2005). Hemodynamic effects of ephedra-free weight-loss supplements in humans. *Am J Med, 118*(9), 998-1003.

Hartman, J. W., Tang, J. E., Wilkinson, S. B., Tarnopolsky, M. A., Lawrence, R. L., Fullerton, A. V., et al. (2007). Consumption of fat-free fluid milk after resistance exercise promotes greater lean mass accretion than does consumption of soy or carbohydrate in young, novice, male weightlifters. *Am J Clin Nutr, 86*(2), 373-381.

Heaney, R. P. (2003). Normalizing calcium intake: Projected population effects for body weight. *J Nutr, 133*(1), 268S-270S.

Heart Protection Study Collaborative Group. MRC/BHF Heart Protection Study of antioxidant vitamin supplementation in 20 536 high-risk individuals: A randomized placebo-controlled trial. *The Lancet*, 2002: 360 (9326): 23-33.

Heymsfield, S. B., Allison, D. B., Vasselli, J. R., Pietrobelli, A., Greenfield, D., & Nunez, C. (1998). Garcinia cambogia (hydroxycitric acid) as a potential antiobesity agent: A randomized controlled trial. *JAMA, 280*(18), 1596-1600.

Jacobsen, R., Lorenzen, J. K., Toubro, S., Krog-Mikkelsen, I., & Astrup, A. (2005). Effect of short-term high dietary calcium intake on 24-h energy expenditure, fat oxidation, and fecal fat excretion. *Int J Obes (Lond), 29*(3), 292-301.

Jewell, D. E., Toll, P. W., Azain, M. J., Lewis, R. D., & Edwards, G. L. (2006). Fiber but not conjugated linoleic acid influences adiposity in dogs. *Vet Ther, 7*(2), 78-85.

Kalman, D., Colker, C. M., Wilets, I., Roufs, J. B., & Antonio, J. (1999). The effects of pyruvate supplementation on body composition in overweight individuals. *Nutrition, 15*(5), 337-340.

Kalman, D., Feldman, S., Martinez, M., Krieger, D., & Tallon, M. (2007). Effect of protein source and resistance training on body composition and sex hormones. *J Int Soc Sports Nutr, 4*(4).

Kaminsky, L. & Dwyer, G. (2006). Body Composition. In L. Hamm (Ed.), *ACSM's Resource Manual for Guidelines for Exercise Testing and Prescription* (Fifth ed., pp. 195-205). Philadelphia: Lippincott Williams & Wilkins.

Kovacs, E. M., Westerterp-Plantenga, M. S., de Vries, M., Brouns, F., & Saris, W. H. (2001). Effects of 2-week ingestion of (-)-hydroxycitrate and (-)-hydroxycitrate combined with medium-chain triglycerides on satiety and food intake. *Physiol Behav, 74*(4-5), 543-549.

Krenkel, J., St Jeor, S., & Kulick, D. (2006). Relationship of Nutrition to Chronic Disease. In L. Kaminsky (Ed.), *ACSM's Resource Manual for Guidelines for Exercise Testing and Prescription* (Fifth ed., pp. 146-164). Philadelphia, PA: Lippincott Williams & Wilkins.

Krieger, J. W., Sitren, H. S., Daniels, M. J., & Langkamp-Henken, B. (2006). Effects of variation in protein and carbohydrate intake on body mass and composition during energy restriction: A meta-regression 1. *Am J Clin Nutr, 83*(2), 260-274.

Kruskall, L. (2006). Portion distortion: Sizing up food servings. *ACSM's Health & Fitness Journal, 10*(3), 8-14.

Kruskall, L., Johnson, L., & Meacham, S. (2003). Eating disorders and disordered eating—Are they the same? *ACSM's Health & Fitness Journal, 6*(3), 6-12.

Lacroix, M., Bos, C., Leonil, J., Airinei, G., Luengo, C., Dare, S., et al. (2006). Compared with casein or total milk protein, digestion of milk soluble proteins is too rapid to sustain the anabolic postprandial amino acid requirement. *Am J Clin Nutr, 84*(5), 1070-1079.

Larsen, T. M., Toubro, S., & Astrup, A. (2003). Efficacy and safety of dietary supplements containing CLA for the treatment of obesity: Evidence from animal and human studies. *J Lipid Res, 44*(12), 2234-2241.

Larsen, T. M., Toubro, S., Gudmundsen, O., & Astrup, A. (2006). Conjugated linoleic acid supplementation for 1 y does not prevent weight or body fat regain. *Am J Clin Nutr, 83*(3), 606-612.

Layman, D. K., Evans, E., Baum, J. I., Seyler, J., Erickson, D. J., & Boileau, R. A. (2005). Dietary protein and exercise have additive effects on body composition during weight loss in adult women. *J Nutr, 135*(8), 1903-1910.

Lee, I., Cook, N., Gaziano, M., Gordon, D., Ridker, P., Manson, J., Hennekens, C., Buring, J. (2005). Vitamin E in the primary prevention of cardiovascular disease and cancer: The Women's Health Study: A randomized controlled trial. *JAMA, 294*, 56-65.

Liu, S., Ajani, U., Chae, C., Hennekens, C., Buring, J., Manson, J. (1999). Long-term ß-carotene supplementation and risk of type 2 diabetes mellitus: A randomized controlled trial. *JAMA, 282*, 1073-1075.

Luscombe-Marsh, N. D., Noakes, M., Wittert, G. A., Keogh, J. B., Foster, P., & Clifton, P. M. (2005). Carbohydrate-restricted diets high in either monounsaturated fat or protein are equally effective at promoting fat loss and improving blood lipids. *Am J Clin Nutr, 81*(4), 762-772.

Mhurchu, C. N., Dunshea-Mooij, C., Bennett, D., & Rodgers, A. (2005). Effect of chitosan on weight loss in overweight and obese individuals: A systematic review of randomized controlled trials. *Obes Rev, 6(*1), 35-42.

Miller, S. L., Tipton, K. D., Chinkes, D. L., Wolf, S. E., & Wolfe, R. R. (2003). Independent and combined effects of amino acids and glucose after resistance exercise. *Med Sci Sports Exerc, 35*(3), 449-455.

MyPyramid. From www.mypyramid.gov

National Academy of Sciences. From www.nasonline.org

National Eating Disorders Association. From www.nationaleatingdisorders.org

National Heart, Lung, and Blood Institute. From www.nhlbi.nih.gov/

National Library of Medicine. PubMed. From www.pubmed.gov

National Weight Control Registry. From www.nwcr.ws

Nattiv, A., Loucks, A. B., Manore, M. M., Sanborn, C. F., Sundgot-Borgen, J., & Warren, M. P. (2007). American College of Sports Medicine position stand: The female athlete triad. *Med Sci Sports Exerc, 39*(10), 1867-1882.

The Natural Pharmacist. From www.iherb.com

Natural Products Association. From www.naturalproductsassoc.org

Newby, P. K., Muller, D., Hallfrisch, J., Andres, R., & Tucker, K. L. (2004). Food patterns measured by factor analysis and anthropometric changes in adults. *Am J Clin Nutr, 80*(2), 504-513.

Nickols-Richardson, S. M., Coleman, M. D., Volpe, J. J., & Hosig, K. W. (2005). Perceived hunger is lower and weight loss is greater in overweight premenopausal women consuming a low-carbohydrate/high-protein vs high-carbohydrate/low-fat diet. *J Am Diet Assoc, 105*(9), 1433-1437.

Noakes, M., Keogh, J. B., Foster, P. R., & Clifton, P. M. (2005). Effect of an energy-restricted, high-protein, low-fat diet relative to a conventional high-carbohydrate, low-fat diet on weight loss, body composition, nutritional status, and markers of cardiovascular health in obese women. *Am J Clin Nutr, 81*(6), 1298-1306.

NSF International. From www.nsf.org

Office of Dietary Supplements. From ods.od.nih.gov

Phillips, S. M., Tipton, K. D., Aarsland, A., Wolf, S. E., & Wolfe, R. R. (1997). Mixed muscle protein synthesis and breakdown after resistance exercise in humans. *Am J Physiol, 273*(1 Pt 1), E99-107.

Phillips, S. M., Tipton, K. D., Ferrando, A. A., & Wolfe, R. R. (1999). Resistance training reduces the acute exercise-induced increase in muscle protein turnover. *Am J Physiol, 276*(1 Pt 1), E118-124.

Pittler, M. H. & Ernst, E. (2004). Dietary supplements for body-weight reduction: A systematic review. *Am J Clin Nutr, 79*(4), 529-536.

Pittler, M. H. & Ernst, E. (2005). Complementary therapies for reducing body weight: A systematic review. *Int J Obes (Lond), 29*(9), 1030-1038.

Position of the American Dietetic Association, Dietitians of Canada, and the American College of Sports Medicine: Nutrition and athletic performance. (2000). *J Am Diet Assoc, 100*(12), 1543-1556.

Preuss, H. G., Garis, R. I., Bramble, J. D., Bagchi, D., Bagchi, M., Rao, C. V., et al. (2005). Efficacy of a novel calcium/potassium salt of (-)-hydroxycitric acid in weight control. *Int J Clin Pharmacol Res, 25*(3), 133-144.

Rainer, L. & Heiss, C. J. (2004). Conjugated linoleic acid: Health implications and effects on body composition. *J Am Diet Assoc, 104*(6), 963-968, quiz 1032.

Rasmussen, B. B., Tipton, K. D., Miller, S. L., Wolf, S. E., & Wolfe, R. R. (2000). An oral essential amino acid-carbohydrate supplement enhances muscle protein anabolism after resistance exercise. *J Appl Physiol, 88*(2), 386-392.

Rodriguez, N. & Gaine, P. (2007). Get the essentials: Protein in the diets of healthy, physically active men and women. *ACSM's Health & Fitness Journal, 11*(2), 13-17.

Roy, B. D., Fowles, J. R., Hill, R., & Tarnopolsky, M. A. (2000). Macronutrient intake and whole body protein metabolism following resistance exercise. *Med Sci Sports Exerc, 32*(8), 1412-1418.

Roy, B. D., Tarnopolsky, M. A., MacDougall, J. D., Fowles, J., & Yarasheski, K. E. (1997). Effect of glucose supplement timing on protein metabolism after resistance training. *J Appl Physiol, 82*(6), 1882-1888.

Samaha, F. F., Iqbal, N., Seshadri, P., Chicano, K. L., Daily, D. A., McGrory, J., et al. (2003). A low-carbohydrate as compared with a low-fat diet in severe obesity. *N Engl J Med, 348*(21), 2074-2081.

Schoeller, D. A. & Buchholz, A. C. (2005). Energetics of obesity and weight control: Does diet composition matter? *J Am Diet Assoc, 105*(5 Suppl 1), S24-28.

Shekelle, P. G., Hardy, M. L., Morton, S. C., Maglione, M., Mojica, W. A., Suttorp, M. J., et al. (2003). Efficacy and safety of ephedra and ephedrine for weight loss and athletic performance: A meta-analysis. *JAMA, 289*(12), 1537-1545.

St-Onge, M. P. (2005). Dietary fats, teas, dairy, and nuts: Potential functional foods for weight control? *Am J Clin Nutr, 81*(1), 7-15.

Stanko, R. T. & Arch, J. E. (1996). Inhibition of regain in body weight and fat with addition of 3-carbon compounds to the diet with hyperenergetic refeeding after weight reduction. *Int J Obes Relat Metab Disord, 20*(10), 925-930.

Stanko, R. T., Tietze, D. L., & Arch, J. E. (1992a). Body composition, energy utilization, and nitrogen metabolism with a 4.25-MJ/d low-energy diet supplemented with pyruvate. *Am J Clin Nutr, 56*(4), 630-635.

Stanko, R. T., Tietze, D. L., & Arch, J. E. (1992b). Body composition, nitrogen metabolism, and energy utilization with feeding of mildly restricted (4.2 MJ/d) and severely restricted (2.1 MJ/d) isonitrogenous diets. *Am J Clin Nutr, 56*(4), 636-640.

SupplementWatch. From www.supplementwatch.com

Tarnopolsky, M. A., Atkinson, S. A., MacDougall, J. D., Chesley, A., Phillips, S., & Schwarcz, H. P. (1992). Evaluation of protein requirements for trained strength athletes. *J Appl Physiol, 73*(5), 1986-1995.

Thompson, J. & Manore, M. (2006). *Nutrition: An Applied Approach* (MyPyramid Edition ed.). San Francisco, CA: Pearson Education.

Tipton, K. D., Ferrando, A. A., Phillips, S. M., Doyle, D., Jr., & Wolfe, R. R. (1999). Postexercise net protein synthesis in human muscle from orally administered amino acids. *Am J Physiol, 276*(4 Pt 1), E628-634.

Tipton, K. D., Rasmussen, B. B., Miller, S. L., Wolf, S. E., Owens-Stovall, S. K., Petrini, B. E., et al. (2001). Timing of amino acid-carbohydrate ingestion alters anabolic response of muscle to resistance exercise. *Am J Physiol Endocrinol Metab, 281*(2), E197-206.

Tsuzuki, T., Kawakami, Y., Nakagawa, K., & Miyazawa, T. (2006). Conjugated docosahexaenoic acid inhibits lipid accumulation in rats. *J Nutr Biochem, 17*(8), 518-524.

Tsuzuki, T., Kawakami, Y., Suzuki, Y., Abe, R., Nakagawa, K., & Miyazawa, T. (2005). Intake of conjugated eicosapentaenoic acid suppresses lipid accumulation in liver and epididymal adipose tissue in rats. *Lipids, 40*(11), 1117-1123.

United States Department of Agriculture (USDA). From www.usda.gov/

United States Food and Drug Administration. From www.fda.gov

United States Pharmacopeia. From www.usp.org

Vega-Lopez, S., Ausman, L.M., Griffith, J.L., Lichtenstein, A.H. (2007). Interindividual variability and intra-individual reproducibility of glycemic index values for commercial white bread. *Diabetes Care*, 30(6): 1412-1417

Volpe, S. (2007a). Recovery beverages: A review of two recent studies. *ACSM's Health & Fitness Journal, 11*(5), 33-34.

Volpe, S. (2007b). Recovery nutrition. *ACSM's Health & Fitness Journal, 11*(3), 33-34.

Westerterp-Plantenga, M. S., Kovacs, E. M., & Melanson, K. J. (2002). Habitual meal frequency and energy intake regulation in partially temporally isolated men. *Int J Obes Relat Metab Disord, 26*(1), 102-110.

Westerterp-Plantenga, M. S., Lejeune, M. P., & Kovacs, E. M. (2005). Body weight loss and weight maintenance in relation to habitual caffeine intake and green tea supplementation. *Obes Res, 13*(7), 1195-1204.

Westerterp-Plantenga, M. S., Lejeune, M. P., Nijs, I., van Ooijen, M., & Kovacs, E. M. (2004). High protein intake sustains weight maintenance after body weight loss in humans. *Int J Obes Relat Metab Disord, 28*(1), 57-64.

Wilkinson, S. B., Tarnopolsky, M. A., Macdonald, M. J., Macdonald, J. R., Armstrong, D., & Phillips, S. M. (2007). Consumption of fluid skim milk promotes greater muscle protein accretion after resistance exercise than does consumption of an isonitrogenous and isoenergetic soy-protein beverage. *Am J Clin Nutr, 85*(4), 1031-1040.

Woloshin, S. & Schwartz, L. M. (2006). Media reporting on research presented at scientific meetings: more caution needed. *Med J Aust, 184*(11), 576-580.

Zemel, M. B. (2005a). Calcium and dairy modulation of obesity risk. *Obes Res, 13*(1), 192-193.

Zemel, M. B. (2005b). The role of dairy foods in weight management. *J Am Coll Nutr, 24*(6 Suppl), 537S-546S.

Zemel, M. B., Richards, J., Mathis, S., Milstead, A., Gebhardt, L., & Silva, E. (2005). Dairy augmentation of total and central fat loss in obese subjects. *Int J Obes (Lond), 29*(4), 391-397.

Zemel, M. B., Richards, J., Milstead, A., & Campbell, P. (2005). Effects of calcium and dairy on body composition and weight loss in African-American adults. *Obes Res, 13*(7), 1218-1225.

Zemel, M. B., Thompson, W., Milstead, A., Morris, K., & Campbell, P. (2004). Calcium and dairy acceleration of weight and fat loss during energy restriction in obese adults. *Obes Res, 12*(4), 582-590.

Laura J. Kruskall, Ph.D., RD, CSSD, FACSM, is the director of nutrition sciences at UNLV and the director of the Didactic Program in Dietetics and the Dietetic Internship. Her areas of expertise are sports nutrition, weight management, and medical nutrition therapy. Her research interests include the effects of nutrition and exercise interventions on body composition and energy metabolism. In addition to her duties at the university, Dr. Kruskall is a member of the Editorial Board for ACSM's *Health & Fitness Journal*, and is a nutrition consultant for Canyon Ranch SpaClub® and Cirque du Soleil in Las Vegas.

Dr. Kruskall received an M.S. in human nutrition from Columbia University and a Ph.D. in nutrition from Penn State University. She is a fellow of the American College of Sports Medicine (ACSM). In addition, she is a Registered Dietitian, a Board Certified Specialist in Sports Dietetics, and an ACSM Certified Health Fitness Specialist, and holds a certification in adult weight management from the American Dietetic Association.